Conserving the Environment

Other Books of Related Interest:

Opposing Viewpoints Series

Endangered Species

Energy Alternatives

The Environment

Global Resources

Global Warming

Pollution

Current Controversies Series

Alternative Energy Sources

Biodiversity

Conserving the Environment

The Rights of Animals

At Issue Series

How Should America's Wilderness Be Managed?

Is Air Pollution a Serious Threat to Health?

Is the World Heading Toward an Energy Crisis?

Nuclear and Toxic Waste

What Energy Sources Should Be Pursued?

"Congress shall make no law . . . abridging the freedom of speech, or of the press."

First Amendment to the U.S. Constitution

The basic foundation of our democracy is the First Amendment guarantee of freedom of expression. The Opposing Viewpoints Series is dedicated to the concept of this basic freedom and the idea that it is more important to practice it than to enshrine it.

Conserving the Environment

Douglas Dupler, Book Editor

GREENHAVEN PRESS

An imprint of Thomson Gale, a part of The Thomson Corporation

Detroit • New York • San Francisco • New Haven, Conn. • Waterville, Maine • London • Munich

Bonnie Szumski, *Publisher*
Helen Cothran, *Managing Editor*

For more information, contact:
Greenhaven Press
27500 Drake Rd.
Farmington Hills, MI 48331-3535
Or you can visit our Internet site at http://www.gale.com

Articles in Greenhaven Press anthologies are often edited for length to meet page requirements. In addition, original titles of these works are changed to clearly present the main thesis and to explicitly indicate the author's opinion. Every effort is made to ensure that Greenhaven Press accurately reflects the original intent of the authors. Every effort has been made to trace the owners of copyrighted material.

Cover photograph reproduced by permission of Paul A. Souders/CORBIS.

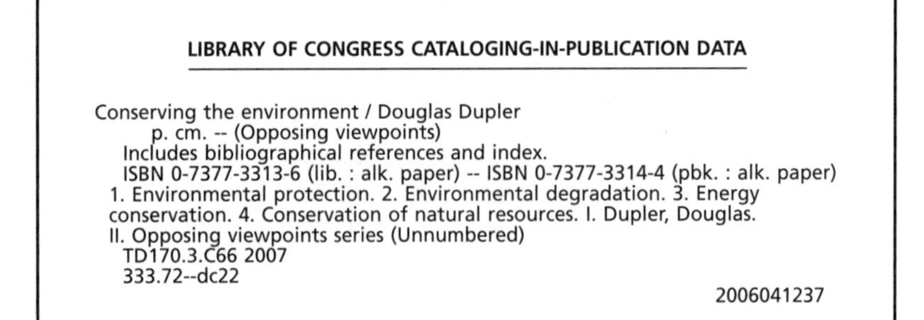
LIBRARY OF CONGRESS CATALOGING-IN-PUBLICATION DATA

Conserving the environment / Douglas Dupler
p. cm. -- (Opposing viewpoints)
Includes bibliographical references and index.
ISBN 0-7377-3313-6 (lib. : alk. paper) -- ISBN 0-7377-3314-4 (pbk. : alk. paper)
1. Environmental protection. 2. Environmental degradation. 3. Energy conservation. 4. Conservation of natural resources. I. Dupler, Douglas. II. Opposing viewpoints series (Unnumbered)
TD170.3.C66 2007
333.72--dc22

2006041237

Printed in the United States of America
10 9 8 7 6 5 4 3 2 1

Contents

Chapter 4: What Can Institutions and Individuals Do to Conserve?

Why Consider Opposing Viewpoints?

> *"The only way in which a human being can make some approach to knowing the whole of a subject is by hearing what can be said about it by persons of every variety of opinion and studying all modes in which it can be looked at by every character of mind. No wise man ever acquired his wisdom in any mode but this."*
>
> *John Stuart Mill*

In our media-intensive culture it is not difficult to find differing opinions. Thousands of newspapers and magazines and dozens of radio and television talk shows resound with differing points of view. The difficulty lies in deciding which opinion to agree with and which "experts" seem the most credible. The more inundated we become with differing opinions and claims, the more essential it is to hone critical reading and thinking skills to evaluate these ideas. Opposing Viewpoints books address this problem directly by presenting stimulating debates that can be used to enhance and teach these skills. The varied opinions contained in each book examine many different aspects of a single issue. While examining these conveniently edited opposing views, readers can develop critical thinking skills such as the ability to compare and contrast authors' credibility, facts, argumentation styles, use of persuasive techniques, and other stylistic tools. In short, the Opposing Viewpoints Series is an ideal way to attain the higher-level thinking and reading skills so essential in a culture of diverse and contradictory opinions.

In addition to providing a tool for critical thinking, Opposing Viewpoints books challenge readers to question their own strongly held opinions and assumptions. Most people form their opinions on the basis of upbringing, peer pressure, and personal, cultural, or professional bias. By reading carefully balanced opposing views, readers must directly confront new ideas as well as the opinions of those with whom they disagree. This is not to simplistically argue that everyone who reads opposing views will—or should—change his or her opinion. Instead, the series enhances readers' understanding of their own views by encouraging confrontation with opposing ideas. Careful examination of others' views can lead to the readers' understanding of the logical inconsistencies in their own opinions, perspective on why they hold an opinion, and the consideration of the possibility that their opinion requires further evaluation.

Evaluating Other Opinions

To ensure that this type of examination occurs, Opposing Viewpoints books present all types of opinions. Prominent spokespeople on different sides of each issue as well as well-known professionals from many disciplines challenge the reader. An additional goal of the series is to provide a forum for other, less known, or even unpopular viewpoints. The opinion of an ordinary person who has had to make the decision to cut off life support from a terminally ill relative, for example, may be just as valuable and provide just as much insight as a medical ethicist's professional opinion. The editors have two additional purposes in including these less known views. One, the editors encourage readers to respect others' opinions—even when not enhanced by professional credibility. It is only by reading or listening to and objectively evaluating others' ideas that one can determine whether they are worthy of consideration. Two, the inclusion of such viewpoints encourages the important critical thinking skill of objectively evaluating an author's credentials and bias. This evaluation will illuminate an author's reasons for taking a particular stance on an issue and will aid in readers' evaluation of the author's ideas.

It is our hope that these books will give readers a deeper understanding of the issues debated and an appreciation of the complexity of even seemingly simple issues when good and honest people disagree. This awareness is particularly important in a democratic society such as ours in which people enter into public debate to determine the common good. Those with whom one disagrees should not be regarded as enemies but rather as people whose views deserve careful examination and may shed light on one's own.

Thomas Jefferson once said that "difference of opinion leads to inquiry, and inquiry to truth." Jefferson, a broadly educated man, argued that "if a nation expects to be ignorant and free . . . it expects what never was and never will be." As individuals and as a nation, it is imperative that we consider the opinions of others and examine them with skill and discernment. The Opposing Viewpoints Series is intended to help readers achieve this goal.

David L. Bender and Bruno Leone,
Founders

Introduction

> *"'Conservation' became 'environmentalism' as concerns extended out of the wilderness areas to broader matters of forest management, agriculture, water and air pollution, nuclear power, and all the other issues we know so well. Environmental concerns and politics have spread worldwide."*
>
> —*Gary Snyder,*
> *writer and conservationist,*
> *in* The Practice of the Wild

The U.S. debate over the environment began in the early 1900s, when the western frontier had been pushed all the way to the coast of California. In the wake of this migration, forests that had once seemed endless had been cleared, and once-abundant species faced extinction. Many nature lovers, such as Sierra Club founder John Muir, became concerned about what was happening to America's wildernesses. This period marks the beginning of the conservation movement.

Muir was one of the first conservationists. A lover of forests and wilderness, Muir succeeded in persuading President Theodore Roosevelt to enlarge the American national park system in the first decade of the 1900s. Muir did not win all his battles, however. Despite his fierce opposition to a proposed dam in California's Yosemite National Park, it was built anyway in order to supply water to San Francisco. This early conservation battle, explains author Rory Spowers in *Rising Tides*, "illustrates the division that has existed ever since between preservation of wilderness *per se* and a managerial approach towards the development of resources." In other words, while some people want land preserved in its natural state, others argue for regulated use of the land for recreation and resource extraction.

The challenge of conserving the environment became more difficult during the first half of the twentieth century, when industrialization changed the American landscape yet again. Many people, especially those living in cities far away from natural areas, gave the environment little thought. Although people complained about air pollution in the cities, pollution was generally tolerated as part of the price of an expanding economy. Anthropologist Wade Davis characterizes the period as one in which environmental concerns were low on most people's lists of things to worry about. According to him, "Simply getting people to stop throwing garbage out of car windows was considered a great environmental victory."

This complacency changed in 1962, when marine biologist Rachel Carson published her book *Silent Spring*. In the book Carson argued that the widespread spraying of pesticides was having harmful effects on the environment as well as contaminating the food supply and threatening human health. The "silent spring" of the book's title referred to the death of birds that Carson claimed was caused by chemical poisoning. The public reacted to Carson's book by calling for a ban on the pesticide DDT, which was thought to weaken the shells of the eggs of many types of birds of prey, thus preventing the eggs from surviving to the hatching stage. The outcry over DDT succeeded in getting the chemical banned.

The social changes of the 1960s brought a new ecological awareness to American culture, galvanizing the environmental movement. Congress passed the Wilderness Act in 1964, which conserved wilderness areas around the country. By 1969 the U.S. government had responded to the public's growing environmental concerns by creating the Environmental Protection Agency (EPA) to monitor pollution and other environmental problems.

The environmental movement gained further ground in the 1970s. On April 22, 1970, an estimated 20 million Americans took part in the first Earth Day. At that time the *New York Review of Books* wrote that the environmental crisis "may indeed constitute the most dangerous and difficult challenge that humanity has ever faced." In the early 1970s President Richard Nixon signed into law the Clean Air Act, the Clean Water Act, and the Endangered Species Act. Americans also began to call for government investment in alternative energy sources.

Under President Ronald Reagan the environmental movement faced serious opposition. Reagan cut the budgets for the EPA and alternative energy development. Those opposed to environmental regulations began the "wise use" movement, which opposed government regulation of public lands. Wise-use advocates argued that public lands should be available for human use, including recreation and resource extraction. Free-market advocates made the case that government control was not the best way to conserve the environment. As economist Richard Stroup writes, "The private sector is often more responsive than government to environmental needs."

The environmental movement became recharged in 1985 when scientists alarmed the world by announcing that they had discovered a hole in the ozone layer of the earth's atmosphere that filters out harmful radiation. Over a decade earlier, it was postulated that chlorofluorocarbons (CFCs), industrial chemicals used in air conditioners and aerosol sprays, could damage the ozone. By 1987 the ozone hole was the size of North America. That same year the first global environmental treaty—called the Montreal Protocol—was signed. It required countries around the world to phase out the use of CFCs. In the late 1980s the issue of global warming received worldwide attention. In 1988 the World Meteorological Organization and the United Nations Environmental Programme formed the Intergovernmental Panel on Climate Change (IPCC) to study global warming.

Concern over global warming continued during the 1990s. In 1997, in response to scientific reports about the threat of global warming, the nations of the world convened in Japan and crafted the Kyoto Protocol, an international agreement to limit greenhouse gas emissions. The administration of President Bill Clinton agreed to the protocol, but the United States backed out of the treaty under President George W. Bush in 2001.

The U.S. environmental movement that started with John Muir in the early twentieth century is now more than a century old. During its history environmentalists have won and lost many battles, but despite the sporadic nature of their achievements, conservationists continue to work for environmental protections. The authors in *Opposing Viewpoints: Conserving the Environment* address some of the environmental issues of the twenty-first century in the following chapters: Is There an Environmental Crisis? What Energy Sources Can Conserve the Environment? How Can Natural Resources Be Conserved? What Can Institutions and Individuals Do to Conserve? As the authors show, balancing environmental concerns with economic needs continues to fuel debate about how best to protect species and habitats—including our own.

Chapter 1

What is the Extent of Environmental Problems?

Chapter Preface

One of the measures used to determine the state of the environment is the amount of human-made pollutants found in organisms and ecosystems. The Environmental Protection Agency (EPA) reports that there are about eighty thousand human-made chemicals produced in the United States. In its report *Toxic Release Inventory*, prepared in 2000, the EPA estimates that about 7.1 billion pounds of hazardous compounds were released into the air and water that year. In January 2003 the U.S. Centers for Disease Control and Prevention (CDC) released the *Second National Report on Human Exposure to Environmental Chemicals*, which cataloged the over one hundred chemicals found in people's bodies. Among the chemicals tested for are pesticides, disinfectants, plastic byproducts, and heavy metals such as mercury. For many experts, determining whether or not the environment is in jeopardy requires measuring the extent of these chemical pollutants.

Many environmentalists are certain that chemicals produced by America's factories are contaminating people. Jane Houlihan of the Environmental Working Group argues that there is "irrefutable proof that humans carry around scores of industrial chemicals, most of which have never been tested for human health effects." As environmental medicine specialist Michael Lerner claims, "The simple truth is that we are now all holding body burdens of these chemicals."

Not everyone agrees with these assessments, however. Many experts assert that the U.S. government has regulations in place to guarantee Americans' safety. The American Chemistry Council (ACC), in a statement issued in response to the CDC report, contends that "chemicals are evaluated by government scientists before being used, and there are precautions in place to help keep us safe from both natural toxins and modern chemicals." Others argue that no studies have proven that the presence of chemicals in the body actually poses a health risk. According to Colin Humphris of the European Chemical Industry Council, "The proof for a link between the presence of chemicals in blood and health is extraordinarily tenuous.... Just the presence of some substance doesn't mean there is a health risk."

The controversy over chemicals will likely continue because the health effects of synthetic chemicals in the environment can be difficult to determine. Some chemicals show up in the body in such minute amounts that they are difficult to study. Especially difficult to determine are the health effects of long-term exposure. Studies may need to be performed over many decades until scientific certainty over health and environmental effects can be reached. Because it can be difficult to determine the nature and scope of environmental threats such as toxic chemicals, the controversy over the state of the environment will likely continue well into the future. The authors in the following chapter explore the extent of other environmental problems and whether they are serious enough to warrant government attention.

VIEWPOINT

> *"Our globalized corporate empire menaces the future of the entire biosphere."*

The Earth Faces an Environmental Crisis

Kenny Ausubel

Kenny Ausubel is an award-winning journalist, an entrepreneur, and the founder of Bioneers, a group dedicated to earth-friendly business concepts. He is also the author of Restoring the Earth: Visionary Solutions from the Bioneers. *In this viewpoint Ausubel argues that the world environment is approaching collapse. He claims that recent catastrophic fires, floods, and insect infestations are due to widespread environmental destruction. However, Ausubel believes that people have the tools to solve environmental problems.*

As you read, consider the following questions:

1. What evidence does Ausubel provide to prove there is an environmental crisis?
2. According to this viewpoint, how should societies treat the free market business model?
3. What role does the author believe that the government should take in solving environmental problems?

For all the chatter about the Age of Information, we really seem to be entering the Age of Biology. We didn't invent nature. Nature invented us. Nature bats last, as the saying goes and, more importantly, it's her playing field. We would do well to learn at least some of the ground rules. . . .

Life is intimacy interconnected. As a culture we've made a basic systems error to believe that we exist somehow separate from nature, or from one another. That illusion could prove fatal at this momentous cusp, this time at which our turbo-charged technologies and overwhelming numbers have given us, for the first time in history, the capacity to blow it on a planetary scale.

Our globalized corporate empire menaces the future of the entire biosphere. Empires are castles made of sand: They always crumble, they always fade away. But by the time this empire strikes out, the biological game could be all but over. Corporate globalization is killing off its host—and ours. Gary Larsen once did a cartoon in which a ship is sinking, and a pack of dogs crowded into a lifeboat are watching it go down. The lead dog says to the others, "OK—all those in favor of eating all the food all at once, raise your paws." That's economic globalization in a nutshell.

Fall of Ancient Civilizations

The real-world situation that is spontaneously combusting today is a perfect storm of extreme environmental degradation and rolling infrastructure collapse. It is by no means the first time this has happened. Previous civilizations have slid into ruin through self-induced environmental catastrophe, but in the past the damage has always been localized.

As [author] Jared Diamond pointed out in *Guns, Germs, and Steel*, these societies met their demise by cutting down forests, eroding topsoil and building burgeoning cities in dry areas that eventually ran short of water. Sometimes hastened by sudden climate change, the ensuing disintegration occurred suddenly—in a matter of a decade or two after a society reached its peak of population, wealth and power. Because that pinnacle also marked maximum resource consumption and waste production, it produced unsupportable environmental impacts.

But there's more to it, Diamond says. "They had foolish leaders . . . who embroiled them in destabilizing wars and didn't pay attention to problems at home. They were overwhelmed by desperate immigrants, as one society after another collapsed, sending floods of economic refugees to tax the resources of the societies that weren't collapsing."

When Diamond studied the ecological downfall of Mexico's ancient Mayan civilization, he determined that the final strand in its unraveling was a crisis of political leadership. "Their [leaders'] attention was evidently focused on the short-term concerns of enriching themselves, waging wars, erecting monuments, competing with one another, and extracting enough food from the peasants to support all these activities." Sound familiar, fellow peasants?

A Reeling Planet

Today we're going *mano a mano* [hand to hand] with the whole biosphere, and she's responding with her own form of deregulation. The planet is reeling from record-smashing temperatures, violent storms, long-term droughts, hundred-year floods, unstoppable fires, massive insect infestations, migrating disease patterns, rising seas, and a level of species extinctions not seen in 65 million years. Twelve thousand people died in France this summer [2003] from record-setting heat. In Phoenix, Arizona, people's flip-flops melted on the pavement. One woman who tripped and fell face-first on the sidewalk was rushed to a burn unit. And global warming is just getting going.

Last year [2002], the White House pressured the EPA [Environmental Protection Agency] to hit the delete key in its state-of-the-environment report regarding the forty-weight connection between global warming and the burning of fossil fuels. The US political class says we need more scientific study while they march us backwards into the 21st century dragging sacks of coal behind them. But the science is unequivocal: It's no longer a matter of connecting the dots. It's a matter of connecting the elephants in the room.

Global warming means more and bigger storms, and one of the most striking images from the relatively mild Hurricane Miserabel Isabel was the battered mall of the Washington Monument. A large stand of flagpoles forlornly flew the stars and stripes, shredded to tatters by the violent weather. As the great urban farmer Michael Abelman said, "After all, what good is a country and a flag if there is no more fertile soil, no ancient forests, no clean water, no pure food? If you really love your country, protect and restore some wildness. Support local agriculture. Plant a garden. Those who work to protect and restore these things are the real patriots."

In truth, the US political class is clueless. Its only plan is to eat all the food all at once. Although the empire may seem awesomely powerful, it's coming apart at the seams.

New Solutions

But what is also true here and around the world is that people are stepping up with real solutions. There's a new superpower: Global popular movements. They are growing from the bottom up, taking back control over our lives, our communities, our economies and our cultures. People are again starting to assume responsibility for the lands, the waters, the forests, and the global commons we all share.

People worldwide are rejecting the deification of the market over environmental and human rights. As Amory Lovins has said, "Markets make a great servant but a bad master and a worse religion. . . . And a society that tries to substitute markets for politics, ethics, or faith is seriously adrift."

Wayne Stayskal. Reproduced by permission.

There are brilliant scientific and social innovators among us who've been patiently incubating the seeds of successful local, regional, and even societal plans for the transformation to a sustainable civilization. An alternative globalization movement of unprecedented proportions is taking shape, weaving a green web of innovative models grounded in true biotechnologies and social equity.

This new world is being born right now before our eyes. It mimics the decentralized intelligence of living systems, the innate democracy of life. It's founded in the recognition that the first homeland security comes from environmental security. Our civilization's out-of-body experience is screeching to a halt as we awaken to our absolute dependence on natural life-support systems and our interdependence with all life.

Governmental Help

In a world where half the people live on $2 a day or less, we can have no peace. The world's most dangerous political hot spots and breeding grounds for terrorism are exactly the same places with the worst environmental devastation and poverty. Go figure.

We're entering into unknown territory. There will be little to hold onto. It could be a time of unimaginable suffering and loss. But it will also be a renaissance of flourishing creativity and deep healing. The regenerative capacity of nature is powerful beyond our imagination. And the boundless nobility of the human soul is arising everywhere in waves of caring and kindness. Our social security is being woven in community, as people gather to mend our shredded social fabric and solve problems together. There is as much cause for hope as for horror. And we know we must prevail.

We can start by attending to our worst wounds. In very practical terms, the solution is to invest in our problems. We need a Green New Deal, a massive global investment in repairing the environment, transforming our infrastructures, and restoring people. The measure of any solution is whether it solves for pattern by resolving multiple problems in one fell swoop.

What's called for is strong government leadership to reboot the system. We need an immediate global Marshall plan of clean, renewable energy, and the re-design and rebuilding of our decaying infrastructures and clotted transportation systems. We can jump-start a permanent transition to an ecological agriculture that produces healthy, nutritious food in regionalized foodsheds—restores the land, air and water—and revives rural economies thriving with small and medium-sized farms. We need a just legal system that puts human and environmental rights above corporate rights. All these programs will yield dramatically positive results—environmentally, economically, socially and spiritually. And all of it is attainable.

> *"If you value clean air, clean water, and wilderness, you've got good reasons to celebrate."*

The Earth Does Not Face an Environmental Crisis

Joseph Bast

Joseph Bast is the president of the Heartland Institute, a think tank dedicated to free market solutions to environmental and social problems. He is the coauthor of the book Eco-Sanity: A Common-Sense Guide to Environmentalism. *In this viewpoint Bast claims that the state of the environment has been improving. He contends that environmentalists exaggerate threats to the environment in order to garner contributions to their organizations. Private companies, not governments, are most effective in protecting the environment, he maintains.*

As you read, consider the following questions:

1. What trends in air pollution does Bast refer to?
2. According to the author, why does "zero tolerance" for pollution not make sense?
3. How is privatization defined in this viewpoint?

Joseph Bast, "Common-Sense Environmentalism," *Intellectual Ammunition*, September 1, 2002. Reproduced by permission.

Between the eco-catastrophists on the left and corporate apologists on the right are the rest of us.

We want a clean and safe environment, but we're not convinced we have to surrender our civil and economic liberties to achieve it. We want government to step in and protect water and air quality, but we don't necessarily trust government to always do the job well, and certainly not efficiently. We don't trust corporations, but we know we depend on them for jobs and the high standard of living we enjoy. . . .

I believe you can be a good environmentalist without falling for every hyped-up "crisis of the month," and also without tolerating pollution or ignoring evidence of environmental and human health hazards. In other words, there is a common-sense environmentalism for those of us stuck in the middle that avoids the hype of the left and the denial of responsibility by the right and still makes sense.

Not on the Eve of Destruction

The first principle of Common-Sense Environmentalism is that we are not on the eve of destruction. Most people by now have heard that air, water, food, and working conditions in the United States have all become cleaner and safer over time, not more polluted or dangerous. Let's look at some numbers.

- Total air pollution emissions in the U.S. fell 34 percent between 1970 and 1990, and today [late 2002] are lower than they were in 1940, some 62 years ago. During the 1990s, the number of "bad air" days—when air quality falls below federal air quality standards—fell 76 percent in Boston, 78 percent in Chicago, 54 percent in Los Angeles, and 88 percent in San Diego.
- Water quality—measured by miles of rivers and percentage of lakes that are drinkable and swimmable—is up around the country, and in some cases dramatically so. Sports fishing has returned to all five of the Great

Happy Earth Day 2005

Just in time for Earth Day, the American Enterprise Institute and the Pacific Research Institute released their annual *Index of Leading Environmental Indicators 2005*. The 2005 *Index* looks at trends in air and water quality, the amount of toxic materials being released into the environment, and forest growth in the United States. Some the best news is on air quality trends. The *Index* finds that "air pollution fell again in the United States to its lowest level ever recorded." The Environmental Protection Agency (EPA) reports that since 1976, when national measuring began, levels of ozone in the air have dropped 31 percent, sulfur dioxides are down 72 percent, nitrogen dioxide was cut by 42 percent, carbon dioxide plunged 76 percent, and particulates (smoke and dust) fell by 31 percent. . . .

Lake Erie is no longer "*dead* "; the Potomac, which in the 1960s was lined with signs warning against coming into contact with the water, now has beavers swimming under the Key Bridge connecting Roslyn and Georgetown; and the Cuyahoga River, which infamously *caught fire*, is now an upscale riverfront dining and entertainment district.

Ronald Bailey, "Happy 35th Earth Day,"
Reason Online, *2005. www.reason.com.*

Lakes; the number of fishing advisories has fallen; and a debate has started concerning the scientific basis of many of the remaining advisories.

- The average annual wood growth in the U.S. today is an amazing three times what it was in 1920. Wildlife populations are recovering, with populations of bald eagles, alligators, white-tailed deer, big horn sheep, elk, and wild turkeys all booming.

If you value clean air, clean water, and wilderness, you've got good reasons to celebrate. But what about global warming, ozone depletion, or cancer-causing chemicals in our food and water? In each case, there is compelling evidence that what you read in fundraising letters from environmental groups and the page-one horror stories in daily newspapers is simply wrong.

- NASA's [National Aeronautics and Space Administration] own satellites do not show a pattern of global warming during the past two decades. A large and growing number of scientists believe the models used to predict global warming are unreliable.
- The amount of ozone depletion that might be caused by man-made chemicals is a tiny fraction of the day-to-day and season-to-season flux in ozone levels that occurs naturally. So small are the possible effects of ozone depletion that it is hardly conceivable we will ever be able to measure them.
- Former Surgeon General C. Everett Koop said "consumer advocates, however well intentioned, continue to tell us that dangerous, cancer-causing pesticides are present in our food and that we and our children are at extreme risk. This is simply not true. There is no food safety crisis."

Environmentalists Must Change

Many of the most obvious and easiest-to-control sources of pollution have now been dealt with. Factories account for a very small and declining share of air and water pollution, for example. The pollution that remains is usually from diverse and often difficult-to-find sources of pollution.

Heavy-handed, top-down government regulation is not likely to be effective at solving environment problems in the twenty-first century. We need a new approach, one that recognizes that problems have changed. Old approaches such as "zero tolerance" don't make sense when new technology allows us to measure the presence of chemicals in parts per *trillion.*

First, we have to *leave behind the scare tactics* and emotional appeals that dominate the environmental movement today. Most environmentalists rely on fundraising letters from groups such as the Sierra Club and Greenpeace for just about everything they think they know about protecting the environment. In truth, this "crisis of the month" approach is just a *direct mail scam* aimed at scaring people into making contributions.

Second, we need new ways to *tap the dispersed knowledge* individuals have about their local environment. There are enormous opportunities to improve environment protection simply by removing tax and regulatory barriers to innovation and local stewardship and ending subsidies to activities that are environmentally destructive.

Third, we need to *prioritize* problems, admitting some are more serious than others, and admitting also that we have limited time and resources to invest in environmental protection. We might as well get the most "bang for the buck" by addressing real, rather than imaginary, problems. That's all "cost-benefit analysis" means. It's a good idea.

Private Sector Is a Reliable Ally

Radical environmental groups denounce the very idea of relying on the private sector to protect the environment, but it should be no more controversial than having a private company collect your garbage or repair potholes in your street.

Privatization— shifting goods and services out of the public sector and into the private sector—has spread to every corner of the globe. Nine out of ten municipalities in the U.S. now use private businesses to manage their parks or water treatment facilities or provide janitorial, accounting, or some other service. Over 90 percent report that contracting out saves them money, produces a higher quality of service, or both.

In the private sector, business owners have an equity stake in getting the job done on time and under budget. If they can find a way to reduce costs or produce a better service, they earn more money. If they don't, a smarter competitor will take business away from them. In the public sector, bureaucrats don't have an equity stake in their departments or agencies, and if they fail to keep costs under control, there is no competitor out there to which disappointed customers can switch.

Markets are able to tap the dispersed knowledge and incentives of individuals by *motivating* people to do the right thing. It is only common sense that it is easier to get someone to do something he wants to do, than it is to force someone to do what he doesn't want to do. The first way is the market's way; the second way is relying on government.

When the iron curtain fell in Eastern Europe, we witnessed environmental devastation on a previously unknown scale. The end of the Cold War helped demonstrate that government—even omnipotent government—does a poor job exercising stewardship over the environment when "everyone" owns the air, water, and wilderness areas.

For people sincerely committed to the goals of a cleaner and safer environment, these are truly the best of times. The air we breathe, the water we drink, and the food we eat are all safer than at any previous time in our lives. Wilderness areas in the United States are expanding, wildlife is flourishing, and once-endangered species have been saved.

We now know that prosperity, private property rights, and freedom from an overly intrusive government, all values that we share, need not be sacrificed to save the environment. We can have them all, but it requires a new approach to environmentalism that relies more on science and less on hype.

VIEWPOINT 3

> *"Seen in its full dimensions, the challenge of global climate change seems truly overwhelming."*

Global Warming Poses a Serious Threat

Ross Gelbspan

Ross Gelbspan is a Pulitzer Prize–winning journalist and the author of two books on global warming and climate change. In this viewpoint he contends that scientists have adequately proved that humans are causing global warming by burning fossil fuels. He claims that global warming will damage the environment and human societies unless the world transitions to using renewable and nonpolluting energy sources such as wind and solar power. This viewpoint is excerpted from Gelbspan's book, Boiling Point: How Politicians, Big Oil and Coal, Journalists, and Activists Are Fueling the Climate Crisis—and What We Can Do to Avert Disaster.

As you read, consider the following questions:

1. By what percentage must the use of coal and oil be reduced, as argued by Gelbspan?

Ross Gelbspan, *Boiling Point: How Politicians, Big Oil and Coal, Journalists and Activists are Fueling the Climate Crisis—and What We Can Do to Avert Disaster*, New York, NY: Basic Books, 2004.

2. According to Gelbspan, in what year did scientists declare that global warming is caused by human activity?
3. How many people, according to this viewpoint, died during Europe's 2003 heat wave?

By late 2003, the signals were undeniable: Global climate change is threatening to spiral out of control.

The six-month period from June to December 2003 brought a succession of scientific findings, climate impacts, political and diplomatic developments, and responses from the financial world that vividly underscored the urgency and magnitude of the climate crisis.

The events of that year surprised even many seasoned climate scientists—and brought home to many others the fact that, given all its ramifications, the climate crisis is far more than just an environmental issue. It is a civilizational issue.

Nevertheless, by the end of 2003, most Americans were still in denial.

The evidence is not subtle. It is apparent in the trickling meltwater from the glaciers in the Andes Mountains that will soon leave many people on Bolivia's mountainside villages with no water to irrigate their crops and, after that, not even enough to drink. It is visible in the rising waters of the Pacific Ocean that recently prompted the prime minister of New Zealand to offer a haven to the residents of the island nation of Tuvalu as it slowly goes under. It is evident in the floods that, in 2002, inundated whole cities in Germany, Russia, and the Czech Republic. It is underscored in the United States by the spread of West Nile virus to forty-two states—and to 230 species of birds, insects, and animals—and in the record-setting 412 tornadoes that leveled whole towns during a ten-day span in May 2003. Its reality is visible from outer space—where satellites have detected an increase in the radiation from greenhouse gases—to our own backyards.

Seen in its full dimensions, the challenge of global climate change seems truly overwhelming. In the absence of a compelling and obvious solution, the most natural human tendency is simply not to want to know about it.

A Crisis of Denial

When a crisis becomes so apparent that denial is no longer tenable, the typical response is to minimize the scope of the problem and embrace partial, inadequate solutions. Witness the voluntary approach of the Bush administration as well as the low goals of the Kyoto Protocol which calls for industrial countries to cut their aggregate emissions by 5.2 percent below 1990 levels, by 2012. (The goal for the United States under the treaty was reductions of 7 percent below 1990 levels.)

By contrast, the science is unambiguous: To pacify our increasingly unstable climate requires humanity to cut its use of coal and oil by 70 percent in a very short time. The grudging response in the United States, and to a lesser extent, abroad, reflects more than a profound underestimation of the scope and urgency of the problem. It betrays an equivalent underestimation of the truly transformative potential of an appropriate solution. Given the scope of the challenge, a real solution to the climate crisis seems to offer a historically unique opportunity to begin to mend a profoundly fractured world.

But it all begins with the climate—and the stunningly rapid atmospheric buildup of carbon dioxide emissions from our fossil fuels. This is trapping growing amounts of heat inside our atmosphere, heat that has historically radiated back into space.

Unintentionally, we have set in motion massive systems of the planet (with huge amounts of inertia) that have kept it relatively hospitable to civilization for the last 10,000 years. With our burning of coal and oil, we have heated the deep oceans. We have reversed the carbon cycle by more than 400,000 years. We have loosed a wave of violent and chaotic weather. We have altered the timing of the seasons. We are living on an increasingly precarious margin of stability.

Two Recent Studies

The accelerating rate of climate change is spelled out in two recent studies—one on the environmental side, one on the energy side.

In 2001, researchers at the Hadley Center, Britain's main climate research institute, found that the climate will change 50 percent more quickly than was previously assumed. That is because earlier computer models calculated the impacts of a warming atmosphere on a relatively static biosphere. But when they factored in the warming that has already taken place, they found that the rate of change is compounding. Their projections show that many of the world's forests will begin to turn from sinks (vegetation that absorbs carbon dioxide) to sources (vegetation that releases carbon dioxide)—dying off and emitting carbon—by around 2040.

The other study, from the energy side, is equally troubling. Three years ago [in 2001], a team of researchers reported in the journal *Nature* that unless the world is getting half its energy from noncarbon sources by 2018, we will see an inevitable doubling—and possible tripling—of atmospheric carbon levels later in this century. In 2002, a follow-up study by many of the same researchers, published in the journal *Science*, called for a Manhattan-type crash project to develop renewable energy sources—wind, solar, and hydrogen fuel. Using conservative estimates of future energy use, the researchers found that within fifty years, humanity must generate at least three times more energy from noncarbon sources than the world currently produces from fossil fuels to avoid a catastrophic buildup of atmospheric CO_2 later in this century.

World Climate Science

For nearly a decade after it surfaced as a public issue in 1988, climate change was regarded primarily as a remote, almost fu-

Hurricanes and Global Warming

Super-powerful hurricanes now hitting the United States are the "smoking gun" of global warming, one of Britain's leading scientists believes.

The growing violence of storms such as Katrina, which wrecked New Orleans, and Rita, now threatening Texas, is very probably caused by climate change, said Sir John Lawton, chairman of the Royal Commission on Environmental Pollution. Hurricanes were getting more intense, just as computer models predicted they would, because of the rising temperature of the sea, he said. "The increased intensity of these kinds of extreme storms is very likely to be due to global warming." . . .

A paper by US researchers last week [September 2005] in the US journal *Science*, showed that storms of the intensity of Hurricane Katrina have become almost twice as common in the past 35 years.

Although the overall frequency of tropical storms worldwide has remained broadly level since 1970, the number of extreme category 4 and 5 events has sharply risen. In the 1970s, there was an average of about 10 category 4 and 5 hurricanes per year but, since 1990, they have nearly doubled to an average of about 18 a year. During the same period, sea surface temperatures, among the key drivers of hurricane intensity, have increased by an average of 0.5C (0.9F).

Michael McCarthy, The Independent/UK, *September 23, 2005.*

turistic, threat based on an arcane branch of science that depended on the mind-numbing complexity and paralyzing uncertainty of an early generation of computer models whose reliability was too suspect to justify enormous policy changes.

In 1995, the issue gained prominence when the world's community of climate scientists first declared they had detected the "human influence" on the climate. That finding legitimized global climate change as a major environmental issue. As a consequence, climate change was subsequently accorded the same mix of rhetorical concern and political inaction as most other environmental issues.

In 2001, however, the issue was infused with a jolt of urgency. That January, the UN [United Nations] Intergovernmental Panel on Climate Change (IPCC) concluded that the climate is changing far more rapidly than scientists had previously projected.

More than 2,000 scientists from 100 countries, participating in the largest and most rigorously peer-reviewed scientific collaboration in history, reported to the UN that brutal droughts, floods, and violent storms across the planet will intensify because emissions from humanity's burning of coal and oil is driving up temperatures much more rapidly than scientists had anticipated just six years earlier.

"The most comprehensive study on the subject [indicates] that Earth's average temperature could rise by as much as 10.4 degrees over the next 100 years—the most rapid change in 10 millennia and more than 60 percent higher than the same group predicted less than six years ago," according to the *Washington Post.*

Floods and Droughts

Rising temperatures will melt ice sheets and raise sea levels by as much as thirty-four inches, causing floods that could displace tens of millions of people in low-lying areas—such as China's Pearl River Delta, much of Bangladesh, and the most densely populated area of Egypt.

Droughts will parch farmlands and aggravate world hunger. Storms triggered by such climatic extremes as El Niño will become more frequent. Diseases such as malaria and dengue fever will spread, the report noted.

A second working group of the IPCC—one that focused on the impacts of coming climate changes—reached the extremely sobering conclusion that "most of earth's inhabitants will be losers," in the words of the group's co-chair, James McCarthy of Harvard University.

The report concluded that poor countries in Africa, Asia, and Latin America with limited resources would bear the brunt of the most extreme climate changes. It added that economic losses from natural catastrophes increased from about $4 billion a year in the 1950s to $40 billion in 1999, with about one-fourth of the losses occurring in developing countries.

(Two years later, nature had already upped the ante. In 2003, the United Nations reported that climate impacts cost the world $60 billion that year, an increase of 10 percent over the $55 billion in climate-related damages in 2002.)

"The scientific consensus presented in this comprehensive report about human-induced climate change should sound alarm bells in every national capital and in every local community. We should start preparing ourselves," declared Klaus Topfer, director of the United Nations Environment Programme (UNEP).

A Bad Year

In the fall of 2003, a succession of events—climatic, economic, and political—coalesced into a vivid mosaic that reflects the reach and variety of climate impacts and their reverberation through our economic and political institutions.

Several developments . . . were particularly ominous because of their scope:

- The entire ecosystem of the North Sea was found to be in a state of collapse because of rising water temperatures.

- For the first time in recorded history, the world consumed more grain than it produced for *four years in a row.* The reason: rising temperatures and falling water tables—both consequences of global climate change.
- The German government declared that the goals of the Kyoto Protocol need to be increased by a factor of four to avoid "catastrophic" changes. Otherwise, the climate will change at a rate not seen in the last million years.
- The most highly publicized impact of global warming in 2003 involved a succession of headlines from Europe about an extraordinary summertime heat wave. . . . When that brutal summer finally subsided, it left more than 35,000 people dead.
- The following month, silently and out of view of most of the world, the biggest ice sheet in the Arctic—3,000 years old, 80 feet thick, and 150 square miles in area—collapsed from warming surface waters in September 2003. The Ward Hunt Ice Shelf, located 500 miles from the North Pole on the edge of Canada's Ellesmere Island, broke in two. A massive freshwater lake long held back by the ice also drained away.
- The same month brought another startling—and largely unanticipated—consequence of our fossil fuel use. Scientists reported that the pH level of the world's oceans had changed more in the last 100 years than it had in the previous 10,000 years—primarily because of the fallout from emissions caused by coal and oil burning. In short, the oceans are becoming acidified.
- By the fall of 2003, an eighteen-month drought in Australia had cut farm incomes in half—and left many scientists speculating that the prolonged drought may have become a permanent condition in one of the country's richest food-growing areas. . . .

The Business Response

Perhaps the strongest response of the financial community to the climate crisis came from one of the world's largest insurers. In May 2003, Swiss Reinsurance announced that it was asking directors and officers of its client companies what their firms were doing to reduce their use of fossil fuels. The company made clear that if those corporate officials were not moving aggressively enough to reduce their carbon emissions, they would risk losing liability insurance.

But if the increasingly visible risks were causing ripples in the financial world, they seemed the subject of an almost perverse kind of satisfaction by the world's largest oil company, ExxonMobil.

In late 2003, the oil giant announced it was anticipating a 50 percent increase in global carbon emissions by the year 2020. "Between now and 2020 we estimate increases of some 3.5 billion tonnes per year of additional carbon emissions, so it's definitely increasing," said Randy Broiles, global planning manager for ExxonMobil's oil and gas production unit. Despite expected increases in energy efficiency, more cars, rising industrial output, and rising living standards in the developing world will create a worldwide demand for about 40 percent more energy in the next two decades, Broiles said.

Unlike the world's community of climate scientists and most of the world's governments, ExxonMobil stands to benefit from the coming surge in carbon emissions. "The oil resource base is huge—it's huge," Broiles told a conference, "and we expect it to satisfy world demand growth well beyond 2020." . . .

Reasons for Hope

But the real news about climate change is not about its destructive potential. The real news lies in the extraordinary opportunity the climate crisis presents to us. Given how very central energy is to our existence, a solution to climate change—which is appropriate to the magnitude of the problem—could also begin to reverse some very discouraging and destructive political and economic dynamics as well.

Nature's requirement that humanity cut its use of carbon fuels by 70 percent in a very short time leaves us with basically two choices. We can either regress into a far more primitive and energy-poor lifestyle—or we can mount a global project to replace every oil-burning furnace, every coal-fired generating plant, and every gasoline-burning car with noncarbon and renewable energy sources. A properly framed plan to rewire the globe with solar energy, hydrogen fuel cells, wind farms, and other sources of clean energy would do much more than stave off the most disruptive manifestations of climate change. Depending on how it is structured, a global transition to renewable energy could create huge numbers of new jobs, especially in developing countries. It could turn dependent and impoverished countries into robust trading partners. It could significantly expand the overall wealth in the global economy. It could provide many of the earth's most deprived inhabitants with a sense of personal future and individual purpose.

> *"Warming trends for the next 100 years have been exaggerated."*

Global Warming Does Not Pose a Serious Threat

Sallie Baliunas

Sallie Baliunas is a senior scientist at the George C. Marshall Institute. In this viewpoint Baliunas challenges some of the main points that Ross Gelbspan makes in his book Boiling Point. *In his book Gelbspan claims that global warming is a serious problem and that it is caused by human activities. According to Baliunas, there is insufficient evidence to support the theory that humans cause global warming. She also maintains that there is no scientific consensus on the effects of global warming, if it in fact is occurring.*

As you read, consider the following questions:

1. What evidence does Baliunas give to downplay concern over melting glaciers and ice sheets?
2. According to the author, on what two points of climate research do most scientists agree?
3. What prediction about global temperature increase during the next century is mentioned in this viewpoint?

Ross Gelbspan and I agree about one thing: The Kyoto Treaty, the international greenhouse gas agreement that took effect in February [2005], will not accomplish much. Even if the U.S. ratified the treaty, the resulting cuts in carbon dioxide emissions—about 5 percent below 1990 levels in developed countries during the next seven years—would be far too modest to keep the air's CO_2 content from rising.

Gelbspan and I disagree about the likely consequences of that failure. In *Boiling Point*, the former *Boston Globe* reporter predicts "disaster"—including mega-droughts, monsoons, refugees, a "Northern hemisphere deep freeze," malaria and dengue epidemics, "not even enough [water] to drink," and "far more allergies"—due to "escalating instability of the climate system." . . .

Gelbspan thus exemplifies the M.O. [modus operandi, or mode of action] of climate alarmists who portray the most extreme predictions as mainstream science without noting the uncertainties surrounding them, dismiss objections as financially or politically motivated, and insist there is no choice but to re-engineer the world according to their plan. These strident voices help shape the popular conception of what human-produced greenhouse gases are doing to the planet and what is required to prevent a *Day After Tomorrow* catastrophe. Their approach, which closes off investigation and shuts down debate through scaremongering and ad hominem attacks, is anti-scientific.

Despite his overwrought warnings, Gelbspan is keen to claim the mantle of science. He threads *Boiling Point* with supposedly science-based chapters. . . . Among other things, these chapters depict glacier and ice sheet changes as harbingers of catastrophe. Yet Antarctica, by far the most massive ice sheet on the planet, has on balance gained mass during the period of recent measurements, 1992 to 2003; instrument records show a net cooling trend between 1966 and 2000. (The Antarctic Peninsula has experienced a warming trend during the last several decades, but it represents just 2 percent of the continent's land mass.) Measurements of the mass of the Greenland ice sheet, the largest in the Northern Hemisphere, are uncertain and may indicate slight shrinkage or growth. Thermometer measurements at the summit of the ice sheet show a recent cooling trend in summer, the season of ice melt. Mountain glaciers also tell a complex story; many retreated rapidly in the 19th century, well before the emission of most of the carbon dioxide from energy use. A few maritime glaciers have recently expanded. . . .

How Much Warming?

Gelbspan is also careless in his description of those who disagree with him. He fails to explain that the "greenhouse skeptics" he cites—those "criminals against humanity"—accept that the industrial emission of CO_2 and other greenhouse gases has contributed to a warming trend during the last century. What remains at issue is the extent of this contribution and the magnitude of warming that can be expected during the next century. Computer simulations of uncertain reliability indicate that by 2100 the globally averaged surface temperature will rise approximately 2.5 degrees Celsius, which would seem to require a wholesale switch to nuclear power in the next few decades to avoid the devastation of energy poverty. But other lines of evidence suggest a change of 1 degree or less, which would be comparable to past natural change, making the transition to 21st-century energy technologies much more affordable. *Boiling Point* obscures this ongoing debate by repeatedly appealing to a nonexistent scientific consensus.

Gelbspan portrays dissent from his view of climate change as evidence of the fossil fuel industry's corrupting influence, which apparently extends to scientists, journalists, the current administration, even labor union leaders and environmental activists. Yet *Boiling Point* does not consider the financial,

An Extremist Hoax

I called the threat of catastrophic global warming the greatest hoax ever perpetrated on the American people in a statement, to put it mildly, that was not viewed very kindly by the environmental extremists and their elitist organizations.

I also pointed out in a lengthy committee report that those same environmental extremists exploit the issue for fundraising purposes, raking in millions of dollars, even using Federal taxpayers' dollars to finance the campaigns.

For these groups, the issue of catastrophic global warming is not just a favored fundraising tool. In truth, it is more fundamental than that. Put simply, man-induced global warming is an article of religious faith to the radical far left alarmists.

James M. Inhofe, "An Update on the Science of Climate Change," Senate testimony, January 4, 2004.

ideological, and personal interests that favor alarmism, such as the desire by scientists for more research funding; by activists for more donations, media attention, and political relevance; by journalists for better play and bigger book advances. (Such issues are considered in two books by active climate researchers that also offer succinct scientific reviews of alarmist news reports: *Meltdown*, by Patrick J. Michaels, and *Taken by Storm*, by Christopher Essex and Ross McKitrick.) The existence of nonscientific motives does not tell us which side is right; only careful consideration of the evidence can do that. . . .

A Complex Science

Climate is a complex, dynamic system that involves the oceans, the atmosphere, biota, ice, and land, which interact with each other in multifaceted ways. An accurate computer simulation of climate does not yet exist. Quantitative impacts of natural and anthropogenic influences, of which the enhanced greenhouse effect is one, are works in progress. . . .

Still, there are a couple of points on which scientists, including most skeptics, agree:

1. Surface temperature, measured by thermometers and averaged over the globe, has risen about 0.6 degree Celsius since the mid-to-late 19th century. The record shows three trends: a sharp warming trend until around 1940, no warming trend or a slight cooling trend until the 1970s, and a warming trend beginning in the late 1970s. Note, however, that good measurements with few breaks in the record exist for only about 20 percent of the globe, with most of the southern oceans and Antarctica inadequately sampled. In some locations the 19th century ended a several-centuries-long cold period called the Little Ice Age, the waning of which may explain some of the warming. Moreover, globally averaged temperature is a number of little value in estimating local ecosystem response because temperature change has specific local influences and local effects.
2. The air's carbon dioxide content has increased by approximately a third during the last 200 years. Beyond carbon dioxide, other greenhouse gases (notably methane) have also been emitted by human activities. Put together, the energy added to the air by all human-produced greenhouse gases would be equivalent to increasing the air's carbon dioxide content alone by roughly two-thirds. The increase, though, has not been steady. Most of the gases have been added to the air in the last half-century, so they cannot have driven most of the warming trend observed in the early 20th century. The surface trend in the last decades of the 20th century was about 0.17 degree Celsius per decade. Contrary to Gelbspan, who refers to an "escalating pace of climate change," the warming trend has been steady. . . .

Looking at Recent Studies

Gelbspan also downplays the uncertainties about climate change by citing material that he claims validates his alarmist views. He cites, for example, the science volume of the 2001 Third Assessment Report from the United Nations' Intergovernmental Panel on Climate Change (IPCC). This 881-page tome, a worthy overview of a wide body of work related to climate, counts 637 "authors," excluding reviewers, and says "many hundreds of scientists participated," although many contributed to just a few pages on their areas of expertise. Although reviewed, the science volume cannot be said to have undergone what is commonly meant by peer review. Most nonspecialists consult and quote only the 20-page "Summary for Policymakers" (SPM), which also does not meet those standards.

Gelbspan says a 2001 study from the National Academy of Sciences "not only affirmed the findings of the IPCC but indicated that the IPCC may have even understated the magnitude of some coming impacts." The NAS studied only the SPM. In the words of MIT climatologist Richard Lindzen, one of the NAS study's authors, "The SPM . . . is commonly presented as the consensus of thousands of the world's foremost climate scientists. In fact, it is no such thing. Largely for that reason, the NAS panel concluded that the SPM does not provide suitable guidance for the U.S. government." Lindzen adds, "Our primary conclusion was that despite some knowledge and agreement, the science is by no means settled. . . . [The] SPM has a strong tendency to disguise uncertainty, and conjures up some scary scenarios for which there is no evidence."

Gelbspan also cites the 2000 U.S. National Assessment (USNA), produced by scientists who commendably sought, in their words, to "synthesize, evaluate, and report on what we presently know about the potential climate variability and change for the U.S. in the 21st century." The report used projections from two advanced, computer-based descriptions of climate that were also included in the IPCC report, one from the Hadley Centre in the U.K. and the other from the Canadian Climate Center. The idea was that comparing two models "helps capture a sense of the range of conditions that may be plausible in the future." Compared to several available models, the Canadian one yields more extreme temperature predictions, while the British one yields more extreme precipitation predictions.

In science what sounds plausible makes a good start, but it remains speculation until it survives tests against well-measured reality. Both USNA simulations give inaccurate results for current conditions in the U.S., which has relatively good instrument records. For example, the Great Lakes and Hudson Bay area can be too warm by 5 degrees Celsius in winter, while the Southwest is too cold by 5 degrees in winter. In the Central Plains, simulated summers are too hot by 2 to 6 degrees Celsius. . . .

Exaggerated Trends

Yet Gelbspan dismisses uncertainties in forecasts and implies that some of the scariest effects already have happened. "One of the first signs of early-stage [anthropogenic] global warming," he asserts, "is an increase in weather extremes—longer droughts, more heat waves, more severe storms, and much more intense, severe dumps of rain and snow." Here and elsewhere in the book he cites a string of irrelevant weather disaster stories from around the world. Record-busting weather has to be put in the context of records that are generally too short to say much that is scientifically meaningful. As the summary of the IPCC's Third Assessment Report notes, "Some important aspects of climate appear not to have changed. . . . Changes globally in tropical and extratropical storm intensity and frequency are dominated by inter-decadal to multi-decadal variations, with no significant trends evident over the 20th century." . . .

Along with improved knowledge of multiple influences on the recent surface warming trend have come indications that warming trends for the next 100 years have been exaggerated. One reason is that "story lines" (the IPCC's term) of the energy and social future that feed into climate simulations speculate on the high end of reality. The growth rate of the air's carbon dioxide content, for example, has been constant since approximately 1975 and smaller than that assumed by the IPCC. World population, a factor in energy demand, has been revised downward. In the 2002 U.N. Mid-Value Forecast, population grows to a steady 9 billion people, where it remains from 2050 to 2075, and declines thereafter. The IPCC generally assumes population growth throughout the 21st century to about 11 billion people. Likewise, the IPCC assumes per capita carbon dioxide emission will increase, but it has been declining worldwide, despite economic growth. Economist Davis Henderson and statistician Ian Castles have worked to improve the IPCC story lines. One of their criticisms is that projecting future GDPs [gross domestic products] based on recent exchange rates rather than purchasing power parity leads to overestimates of fossil fuel consumption and therefore of future temperature.

In 2002 NASA climate researcher James Hansen, credited with broadening public concern about the air's increased carbon dioxide content through congressional testimony in 1988, wrote, "It is noteworthy that the current IPCC [greenhouse gas emission] scenarios have a growth rate in the 1990s that is almost double the observed rate," which he said "is consistent with their failure to emphasize data." In 2001 Hansen and a co-researcher had published a study that adjusted the exaggerated emission scenarios. They also considered the impact of technologically achievable reductions in air pollutants such as near-surface ozone and black carbon (soot) that are now recognized as potential warming agents. (A 2005 paper co-authored by Hansen suggests that soot from industry and biomass burning in Eurasia is a significant factor in recent Arctic ice melt.) In the 2001 study, Hansen and his co-author predicted "additional warming in the next 50 years of ¾°C±¼°C." That estimate, which falls near the bottom of the IPCC's forecasts, undercuts alarmism with technological optimism.

"Only 5 percent of native forest still stands in the continental United States."

Deforestation Threatens the Environment

Derrick Jensen and George Draffan

Derrick Jensen is the author of several books on environmental and cultural issues, including Listening to the Land *and* A Language Older than Words. *He is an advocate of forest and river preservation and restoration. George Draffan is a carpenter, environmentalist, and the author of several books including* Railroads and Clearcuts. *In this viewpoint, excerpted from their book* Strangely Like War: The Global Assault on Forests, *the authors state that the forests in the United States and the rest of the world are being destroyed by logging and development. They contend that many regions of the world that used to be forested are now deserts.*

As you read, consider the following questions:

1. According to the authors, how many miles of logging roads have been built in U.S. forests?
2. According to this viewpoint, what is the rate of global forest destruction?

Derrick Jensen and George Draffan, *Strangely Like War: The Global Assault on Forests*. White River, VT: Chelsea Green, 2003.

3. What trend, as noted by the authors, becomes apparent when observing the landscapes of older civilizations?

The forests of the world are in bad shape. About three-quarters of the world's original forests have been cut, most of that in the past century. Much of what remains is in three nations: Russia, Canada, and Brazil. Ninety-five percent of the original forests of the United States are gone.

We don't know how fast the surviving forests are disappearing. We don't know how many acres are cut each year in the United States, nor how much of that is old growth. We have estimates . . . but the paucity of information even on present levels of cutting reveals more than it hides: it reveals how desperately out of control is the whole situation.

The United States Forest Service and the Bureau of Land Management sell trees from public forests—meaning they belong to you—to big timber corporations at prices that often do not even cover the administrative costs of preparing the sales, much less reflect full market value. For example, in the Tongass National Forest in southeastern Alaska, 400-year-old hemlock, spruce, and cedar are sold to huge timber corporations for less than the price of a cheeseburger, and taxpayers pay for the building of the logging roads as well. The Forest Service loses hundreds of millions of dollars a year on its timber-sale programs. In other words, if you pay taxes, you pay to deforest your own land.

If you live in the West, Southwest, South, Northeast, Midwest, Alaska, or anywhere else in the United States where there are or were forests, chances are good you've seen or walked clearcuts, sometimes square mile after square mile, cut, scraped, compacted, and herbicided. You've seen lone trees silhouetted on ridgelines, and you've seen once-dense forests reduced to a handful of trees per acre. You've suspected and later learned that these few trees were left so the Forest Service and big timber corporations could maintain that they did not clearcut this particular piece of ground. And maybe you came back another time and saw that the survivors, too, were gone.

You've probably driven highways lined by trees, then pulled over to look around, only to discover that just like in old westerns, where false fronts hid the absence of real stores, you've been sold a bill of goods: a few yards of trees separate the road from yet more clearcuts. This fringe of trees, which reveals recognition on the part of timber corporations and government agencies that industrial forestry requires public deception, is common enough to have been given a name: the beauty strip.

Do yourself—and the forests—a favor. Next time you fly over a once-forested region on a clear day, look down. Pay attention to the crazy quilt of clearcuts you see below, to the roads linking clearcuts and fragmenting forests, roads that wash out in heavy rains to scour streambeds and destroy fisheries.

Native Forests Are Disappearing

Only 5 percent of native forest still stands in the continental United States. Four hundred forty thousand miles of logging roads run through National Forests alone. (The Forest Service claims there are "only" 383,000 miles, but the Forest Service routinely lies, keeping double books—a private set showing actual clearcuts, and a public set showing some of the same acres as old growth—misleading the public by labeling clearcuts "temporary meadows," reducing the stated costs of logging roads by amortizing them over a thousand years, and so on). That's more road than the Interstate Highway System, enough road to drive from Washington, D.C. to San Francisco one hundred and fifty times. Only God and the trees themselves know how many miles of roads fragment the forests.

The forests of this continent have not always been a patchwork of dwindling and increasingly isolated natural communities. Prior to the arrival of our culture, unbroken forests ran along the entire eastern seaboard, leading to the cliché that a squirrel could have leapt tree to tree from the Atlantic to the Mississippi, never having touched the ground. Today, of course, it could still never touch ground, but instead walk on pavement. Polar bears wandered as far south as the Delaware Bay; martens were "innumerable" in New England; wood bison cruised that region; passenger pigeons passed overhead in flocks that darkened the skies for days at a time; Eskimo curlews did the same; rivers and seas were so full of fish they could be caught by lowering a basket into the water. American chestnuts ran from Maine to Florida so thick on the dry ridgetops of the central Appalachians that when their crowns filled with creamy-white flowers the mountains appeared to be covered with snow. Before European "settlement"—read conquest—of America, there was no such thing as "old growth," no such thing as "native forest," no such thing as "ancient forest," because *all* of the forests were mixed old growth, they were all native, they were all diverse, ancient communities. Difficult as all of this may be to imagine, living as we do in this time of extraordinary ecological impoverishment, all of these images of fecundity are from near-contemporary accounts easy enough to find, if only we bother to look.

International Deforestation

Worldwide, forests are similarly under attack. One estimate says that two and a half acres of forest are cut every second. That's equivalent to two football fields. One hundred and fifty acres cut per minute. That's 214,000 acres per day, an area larger than New York City. Seventy-eight million acres (121,875 square miles) deforested each year, an area larger than Poland.

The reasons for international deforestation are . . . similar to those for domestic deforestation. Indeed, those doing the deforesting are often the same huge corporations, acting under the same economic imperatives with the same political powers.

Apologists for deforestation routinely argue that because pre-conquest Indians sometimes "managed" forests by setting small fires to improve habitat for deer and other creatures, industrial "management" of forests—deforestation—is acceptable as well. But the argument is as false and unsatisfying as the beauty strips, and really serves the same purpose: to divert our attention from deforestation. This is analogous to saying that because someone once clipped a partner's fingernails, it's okay for us to cut those fingers off.

I saw this argument presented again [in 2003] in the *San Francisco Chronicle*, in an op-ed piece by William Wade Keye, past chair of the Northern California Society of American Foresters. He wrote, "Native peoples managed the North American landscape, cutting trees and using fire to perpetuate desirable forest conditions. There is no reason that we cannot equal or better this record of stewardship." Actually, there are many reasons. Indians lived in place, and considered themselves a part of the land; they did not come in as an occupying force and develop an extractive economy. They did not participate in an economy and culture that valued money over life. They were smart enough not to invent chainsaws and fellerbunchers (huge shears on wheels that roll along the ground, severing trees and stacking them into piles). They were smart enough not to invent wood chippers or pulp mills. They were smart enough not to invent an economy that ignored everything but cash. They were smart enough not to invent limited liability corporations. They didn't export mountains of timber overseas. They knew trees and other nonhumans as intelligent beings with precious lives worth considering, and not as cash on the stump, or resources to be managed, or even as resources at all. Their spiritual beliefs did not include commands to "subdue the earth," nor was their cosmology based on the absurd notion that one succeeds in life by outcompeting one's human and nonhuman neighbors.

Industrial Forests

The forest industry says that there are more trees growing in the United States now than in 1920. That may be true, since the twenties saw the end of a timber rampage that denuded the entire eastern seaboard. But they are also counting as trees the millions of sickly, chemically supported seedlings (also known as plantation forests) planted around North America by timber and paper companies. These plants are part of a massive monoculture, and bear little resemblance to the functioning, diverse-species ecosystems that deliver all the services we expect from a forest. Our original natural forest cover is being either destroyed or replaced by these simplified systems, which are merely uniform stands of trees of the same age and species.

David Suzuki, From Naked Ape to Superspecies, *2004.*

And the Indians didn't subdue the earth. There is absolutely nothing in our culture's history to suggest that we can "equal or better this record of stewardship." There is everything in our culture's history and present practices to suggest that the deforestation will continue, no matter the rhetoric of those doing the deforestation, and that ecological collapse will be our downfall, as it has been for earlier civilizations.

The Truth on the Ground

But believe neither us, nor even contemporary accounts of early explorers who wrote of the extraordinary richness of native forests, nor especially the handsomely paid liars of the timber industry and the government. For the truth lies not in what they say, nor even in what we say. The truth lies on the ground. Go out and walk the clearcuts for yourself. Rub the dried soil between your fingertips. Walk the dying streams; listen to the silence in the skies (except for the whine of chainsaws and roar of distant logging trucks). Walk among ancient ones still standing, trees sometimes two thousand years old. Put your hands on their bark, on their skin. Taste the difference in the air. Smell it. Reflect on the beauty of what's still there, and on what has been lost—what has been taken from us. . . .

An Old Pattern of Destruction

When you consider the current landscape of the cradle of civilization—what is now Iraq and environs—what pictures come to mind? If you're like me, the images are of barren plains and even more barren hillsides, goats or sheep grazing on a few scrubby bushes breaking a monotony of light brown dirt. But it was not always so. As John Perlin states in *A Forest Journey: The Role of Wood in the Development of Civilization.* "That such vast tracts of timber grew near southern Mesopotamia might seem a flight of fancy considering the present barren condition of the land, but before the intrusion of civilizations an almost unbroken forest flourished in the hills and mountains surrounding the Fertile Crescent." The trees were cut to build the first great cities and the ships that plied the first great empire. Once the ships were built, wood was imported to make the cities even bigger. Down went the great cedar forests of what is now southwest Turkey, the great oak forests of the southeastern Arabian peninsula, and the great juniper, fir, and sycamore forests of what is now Syria. . . .

Let's move a little west. Picture this time the hills of Israel and Lebanon. I recently asked a man from Israel if his country has trees, and he said, "Oh yes, we have lots of little trees, which we water by hand." This fits with the images that come to mind. Every picture I've seen of the Crucifixion, for example, shows a hilltop devoid of trees. The same is true for most of the pictures I've seen of Palestinian refugee camps, and for Israeli settlements. What happened to the "land of milk and honey" we read about in the Bible? And what about those famous "cedars of Lebanon?" You'll find them only on the Lebanese flag now. The rest are long gone—cut to build temples, cities, and ships, cut for fuel, cooking, metalworking, pottery kilns, and all the trinkets of commerce.

Move west again, to Crete, and then up to Greece, and we see the same stories of trees making way for civilization. Knossos was heavily forested and now is not. Pylos, the capital of Mycenaean Greece, was surrounded by giant pine forests. Melos became barren. The same is true for all of Greece.

When you think of Italy, do you think of dense forests? Italy was once forested. These forests fell beneath the axes of the Roman empire.

Or how about North Africa? Surely not. This land is as barren as the Middle East. But here, once again quoting Perlin, "Berbers fulfilled their duty by felling the dense forest growth for their Arab masters. Such large quantities of wood were shipped from these mountains that the local port was named 'Port of the Tree.'" All to make Egyptian warships.

We could continue with this journey, through France and Britain, across North and South America, into Asia and Africa, but by now you see the pattern.

The Pattern Today

The pattern continues today, accelerating as our culture metastasizes across the globe. Worldwide, forests fall.

As of 1997, Nigeria had lost 99 percent of its native forests. The same was true of Finland and India. China, Vietnam, Laos, Guatemala, Ivory Coast, Taiwan, Sweden, Bangladesh, the Central African Republic, the United States, Mexico, Argentina, Burma, New Zealand, Costa Rica, Cameroon, and Cambodia had all lost at least 90 percent. Australia, Brunei, Sri Lanka, Zaire, Malaysia, and Honduras had lost at least 80 percent. Russia, Indonesia, Nicaragua, Bhutan, and the Congo had lost at least 70 percent. Gabon, Papua New Guinea, Panama, Belize, Colombia, and Ecuador had lost at least 60 percent. Brazil and Bolivia had lost more than half. Chile, Peru, Canada, and Venezuela had lost almost half.

Since 1997, of course, things have gotten much, much worse.

> *"Globally, forest cover has remained remarkably stable over the second half of the twentieth century."*

Deforestation Does Not Threaten the Environment

Bjørn Lomborg

Bjørn Lomborg is a professor of political science and statistics in Denmark. He was named one of the one hundred most influential people in 2004 by Time *magazine, after becoming internationally known after the publication of his book* The Skeptical Environmentalist, *from which the following viewpoint has been taken. In this viewpoint Lomborg analyzes the state of the world's forests. He claims that there are no grounds for concern about deforestation. In fact, according to him, the world's forest cover has remained somewhat stable for the past half century. Lomborg also notes that concerns about rain forest destruction are overstated.*

As you read, consider the following questions:

1. Why, according to Lomborg, is it difficult to estimate forest cover?

2. As listed in this viewpoint, which countries contain most of the world's forests?
3. How much of the Amazon rain forest has been cleared by humans, according to the author?

The forests are another form of renewable resource we may be overexploiting. Many people have a strong feeling that the forests are simply disappearing. A *Time* magazine environmental survey carried the headline: "Forests: the global chainsaw massacre." The World Resources Institute simply calls it: "Deforestation: the global assault continues." . . . This is in keeping with a statement by the WWF's [World Wildlife Federation] international president Claude Martin, who in 1997 called a press conference named Eleventh Hour for World's Forests. Here he said: "I implore the leaders of the world to pledge to save their country's remaining forests now—at the eleventh hour for the world's forests." Equally, he claimed that "the area and quality of the world's forests have continued to decline at a rapid rate." Worldwatch Institute even claims that "deforestation has been accelerating in the last 30 years." But there are no grounds for making such claims. Globally, the overall area covered by forest has not changed much since 1950 [according to data from the United Nations (UN)]. . . . Estimates of the possible future for global forests for the rest of the century . . . [include] very pessimistic estimates [that] show a 20 percent decline, but most scenarios show a constant or even somewhat increasing forest area till 2100.

Of course, it is difficult to determine what actually constitutes forest, because there is a gradual transition from dense rainforest to savanna to bush steppe, in the same way as trees become less tall and stand further apart as one approaches the tree line. It is also extremely difficult to compare Brazilian rainforest with Danish beech woodland or an American plantation. If we nevertheless want to attempt such a comparison [the UN report] contains the best information on the global forest area. It is, however, important to stress that it only provides a general impression of the situation.

Globally, forest cover has remained remarkably stable over the second half of the twentieth century. With the longest data series, global forest cover increased from 30.04 percent of the global land area in 1950 to 30.89 percent in 1994, or an increase of 0.85 percentage points over 44 years. With the somewhat shorter data series from 1961, global forest cover is estimated to have fallen from 32.66 percent to 32.22 percent. That is to say, it has fallen by 0.44 percentage points over the last 35 years or so. The UN carried out two global forest surveys in 1995 and 1997 and evaluated a more limited definition of forest area for the period 1980–90 and 1990–5. The survey found that the area covered by forest had shrunk from 27.25 percent to 25.8 percent, or by 1.35 percentage points, although these figures are vitiated by considerable uncertainty. . . .

Most forest by far is concentrated in a few countries. Russia, Brazil, the US and Canada together have more than 50 percent of the world's forest. Globally there is about two to three times as much forests as cropland.

Forests and History

Since beginning farming, man has been felling woodland to get more land for cultivation. Plato wrote of the Attica heights outside Athens that they resembled "the skeleton of a body wasted by disease" as a result of deforestation.

Europe has lost 50–70 percent of its original forest. Much of the continent's forest was felled in the early Middle Ages, to provide either more agricultural land or firewood. Half of France's forest disappeared between 1000 and 1300. The Black Death wiped out one-third of Europe's population in the middle of the fourteenth century, relieving pressure on the forests, which in many cases grew back again. It was not until the 1500s and 1600s that an ever increasing number of people again put the forests under pressure, and more large areas of it were felled. By 1700, France's forests had been reduced in size by more than 70 percent compared to 1000 CE. In the eighteenth century, however, people became aware of the fact that the forests were a limited resource and that they were important for naval shipbuilding purposes. For this reason forest area in Europe only fell by about 8 percent from 1700 onward.

The US has only lost approximately 30 percent of its original forest area, most of this happening in the nineteenth century. The loss has not been higher mainly because population pressure has never been as great there as in Europe. The doubling of US farmland from 1880 to 1920 happened almost without affecting the total forest area as most was converted from grasslands.

On the other hand, many other regions of the world experienced increased deforestation in the nineteenth century. Latin America became part of the world economy at an early stage and has cleared approximately 20 percent of its forest cover over the last 300 years. Much of it went to make way for sugar and later coffee although a gold and diamond fever, which started in 1690, also helped to clear approximately 2 percent of the forest in Brazil.

Asia, which has long had intensive farming, joined the world economy relatively late. It was not until the American Civil War and the opening of the Suez Canal in 1869 that India began to export cotton on a large scale. All in all, southern Asia and China have lost about 50 percent of their forest cover since 1700. Southeast Asia, on the other hand, has only lost 7 percent over the last 300 years, while Africa and Russia have each lost a little under 20 percent.

Globally it is estimated that we have lost a total of about 20 percent of the original forest cover since the dawn of agriculture. This figure is far smaller than the one so often bandied about by the various organizations. The WWF, for example, claims that we have lost two-thirds of all forests since agriculture was introduced . . . although there is no evidence to support this claim.

Deforestation: A General View

The forests have many advantages to offer. The most obvious of these come from an estimated 5,000 commercial products, mainly construction timber, furniture, paper and firewood. It is estimated that, at the global level, forestry contributes some 2 percent of world GDP [gross domestic product], or more than US$600 billion.

In addition to this, the forests offer recreation for urban-dwellers, they help to prevent soil erosion, which silts up rivers and reservoirs, and they reduce flooding. Finally, the forest is home to many species of animals, especially the rainforest, as will be discussed in the section on biodiversity.

The temperate forests, most of which are in North America, Europe and Russia, have expanded over the last 40 years. On the other hand, quite a lot of tropical forest is disappearing. Tropical forests are home to by far the majority of animal and plant species and by far the largest biomass on the planet. In the tropical rainforest, which is the wet part of the tropical forest, one will often find several hundred species of tree within just a few hundred square kilometers. This is in stark contrast to the boreal forests—in Canada's more than 1,000 square kilometers of boreal forest there are only about 20 different tree species.

In the late 1970s it was feared that half or more of the rainforests would disappear within the next few decades. President Carter's environment report, *Global 2000*, estimated an annual tropical forest loss of between 2.3 percent and 4.8 percent. The well-known biologist Norman Myers estimated as recently as the early nineties that 2 percent of all forest was being destroyed every year and believed that by the year 2000—in just nine years at the time of his prediction—we would have lost about a third of the tropical forest area. Actu-

Global Forest Cover Estimates

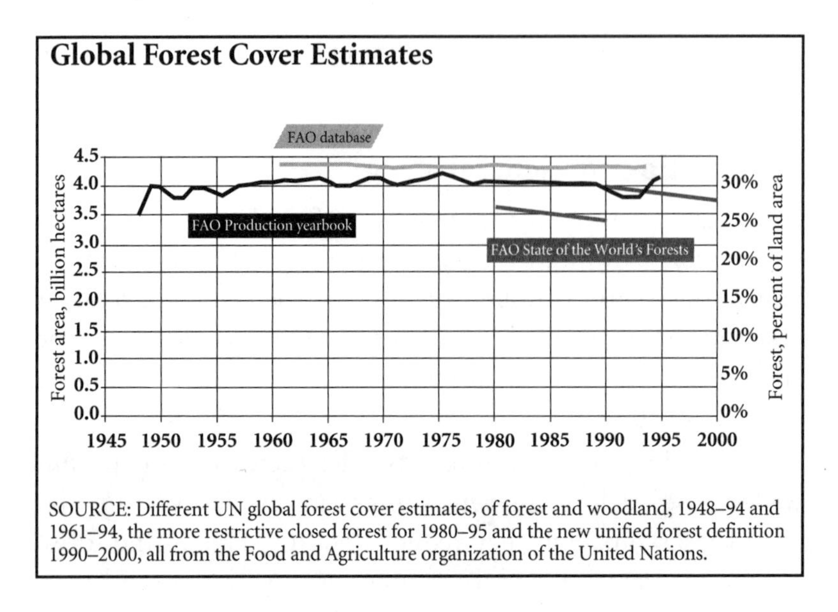

SOURCE: Different UN global forest cover estimates, of forest and woodland, 1948–94 and 1961–94, the more restrictive closed forest for 1980–95 and the new unified forest definition 1990–2000, all from the Food and Agriculture organization of the United Nations.

ally, he claimed that "in just another few decades, we could witness the virtual elimination of tropical forests." Estimates in the same range of 1.5–2 percent were common among biologists. Today we know that these estimates went way over the mark. The usual FAO [Food and Agriculture Organization] estimates put net deforestation in the tropics in the 1980s at 0.8 percent a year, falling to 0.7 percent in the 1990s. With FAO's new 2001-study, based on accurate satellite imagery, the estimate of the net tropical deforestation has declined even further to 0.46 percent. . . .

Deforestation: How Much?

However, in order to evaluate the entire extent of this problem, it is necessary to look at how much tropical forest has actually disappeared. Although precise figures are not available, the Conservation Union World, the IUCN, estimates that 80 percent of the original forest cover is still in place. Within historical times, then, just about 20 percent of all tropical forests has disappeared. Compared with the developed world, where we have cleared almost half of our forest, this is a relatively small figure.

Countries such as Nigeria and Madagascar have admittedly lost well over half their original rainforest, and Central America may have lost 50–70 percent. But overall, they are only home to about 5 percent of the world's tropical forest. Most of it by far is in the Brazilian Amazon. The Brazilian forests make up a third of the world's tropical forest. In comparison, Indonesia—the second largest tropical forest area—"only" has 6 percent of the global total.

In 1988, scientists at Brazil's space agency (INPE) announced that its satellites had located as many as 7,000 fires, and that Brazil was now cutting down 8 million hectares of its forests—some 2 percent—a year. These figures attracted extensive criticism of Brazil for its destruction of irreplaceable nature. It later transpired, however, that these figures had been grossly overstated, and the official preliminary estimate for 1999 was about 1.7 million hectares a year, or just below 0.5 percent a year. In actual fact, overall Amazonian deforestation has only been about 14 percent since man arrived [according to the INPE]. At least some 3 percent of this 14 percent has since been replaced by new forest. . . .

How Much Forest?

If a considered political decision is to be made about how much forest we want to have in the world, it is crucial for us to have a comprehensive view of the arguments for and against exploitation of the forests.

There are two primary reasons for viewing the tropical forests as a vital resource. In the 1970s we were told that rainforests were the lungs of the Earth. Even in July 2000, WWF argued for saving the Brazilian Amazon since "the Amazon region has been called the lungs of the world." But this is a myth. True enough, plants produce oxygen by means of photosynthesis, but when they die and decompose, precisely the same amount of oxygen is consumed. Therefore, forests in equilibrium (where trees grow but old trees fall over, keeping the total biomass approximately constant) neither produce nor consume oxygen in net terms. Even if all plants, on land as well as at sea, were killed off and then decomposed, the process would consume less than 1 percent of the atmosphere's oxygen.

The other argument in favor of preserving the forests is to conserve the globe's profusion of species, or the biodiversity. . . . In short it can be said that over the next 50 years we will not lose 50 percent of all species as claimed by many, but more like 0.7 percent. One cannot generally argue that these species constitute an actual economic resource (along the lines that they may constitute new and potentially vital medicines) but we may well hold moral reasons for their preservation.

At the same time, numerous false impressions exist regarding the condition of our forests. Most people believe that over the last 50 years we have wiped out large swathes of rainforest, and perhaps temperate forest as well. Statements such as the one from the WWF quoted above naturally help to cement this idea. But as we have pointed out, there has not been a fall in global forest area during this period. On the other hand, Europe got rid of a large proportion of its forest by the end of the Middle Ages in order to make room for farming and bigger populations.

Many people also worry that our paper consumption and the use of printed advertising is laying the forests to waste. The Worldwatch Institute wrote in 1998 that "the dramatically increasing demand for paper and other wood products . . . [is] turning local forest destruction into a global catastrophe." But in actual fact, our entire consumption of wood and paper can be catered for by the tree *growth* of just 5 percent of the current forest area.

Periodical Bibliography

The following articles have been selected to supplement the diverse views presented in this chapter.

Centers for Disease Control and Prevention	"National Report on Human Exposure to Environmental Chemicals," July 2005. www.cdc.gov.
Marla Cone	"EPA Is Faulted As Failing to Shield Public from Toxins," *Los Angeles Times*, July 13, 2005.
Michael Crichton	"Environmentalism as Religion," September 15, 2003. www.crichton-official.com.
Herman E. Daly	"Economics in a Full World," *Scientific American*, September 2005.
Environmental Protection Agency	"Toxic Release Inventory (TRI) Program," March 2006. www.epa.gov.
Derrick Z. Jackson	"U.S. Takes Lead in Trashing Planet," *Boston Globe*, April 13, 2005.
Geoffrey Lean	"Global Warming Approaching Point of No Return, Warns Leading Climate Expert," *Independent*, January 23, 2005. www.commondreams.org.
Stacy Malkan	"Pollution of the People," *Multinational Monitor*, May 8, 2003.
Patrick J. Michaels	"Will 2005 Set a Record for Warmth? Does It Matter?" TechCentralStation.com, October 14, 2005. www.tcsdaily.com.
Natural Resources Defense Council	"Healing the Ozone Layer," November 18, 2005. www.nrdc.org.
David Roodman	"Another Take on Free-Market Environmentalism," *PERC Reports*, March 1, 2004. www.heartland.org.

Chapter 2

What Energy Sources Can Conserve the Environment?

Chapter Preface

The possibility of using hydrogen to power homes, businesses, and vehicles has captured widespread attention in the early 2000s. Hydrogen is the most plentiful element in the universe. The burning of hydrogen produces only heat and water—no carbon emissions—making it an attractive option for reducing the pollution that many scientists believe causes global warming. Hydrogen's recent popularity was illustrated when President George W. Bush announced in his 2003 State of the Union address that "the first car driven by a child today could be powered by hydrogen and pollution-free." Transition from dirty fossil fuels to clean-burning hydrogen is one of many proposals for reducing pollution.

Many energy experts and scientists believe that hydrogen should replace fossil fuels as America's main energy source. Jeremy Rifkin, author of *The Hydrogen Economy*, contends that "the switch to a hydrogen economy can end the world's reliance on imported oil." Furthermore, Rifkin argues, the use of hydrogen could move "the world away from a fossil-fuel energy regime . . . [and] mitigate the effects of global warming on the Earth's already beleaguered biosphere." Amory Lovins of the Rocky Mountain Institute, a think tank concerned with energy issues, shares Rifkin's optimism, claiming that "the most likely candidate to power our transportation devices of the future is the simplest, most abundant gas—clean, efficient hydrogen."

Not everyone is optimistic about hydrogen's potential, however. Author Joseph J. Romm is skeptical about the use of hydrogen as a fuel. In his book *The Hype About Hydrogen*, he argues that "the transition to a transportation system based on hydrogen will take decades." Using hydrogen as an automotive fuel is also expensive, he claims. "Unfortunately," Romm writes, "for the foreseeable future, hydrogen cars will almost certainly be unable to compete with alternative strategies for reducing greenhouse gas emissions." Engineering professors Frank Kreith and Ron West explain that "hydrogen is not an energy source. It is only an energy carrier that must be produced from a primary energy source, such as natural gas, coal, nuclear fuel, wind or solar radiation." Thus, critics claim, not only must energy be expended to produce hydrogen, but the fossil fuels used in its production pollute, belying the claim that a transition to hydrogen would benefit the environment.

The debate over hydrogen is likely to continue as experts look for ways to reduce pollution. In the following chapter the authors address other proposals for reducing the emissions that cause global warming.

Viewpoint 1

> *"The good news is that the transition to a sustainable energy future is now underway."*

Renewable Energy Can Help Conserve the Environment

Guy Dauncey

Guy Dauncey is the coauthor, with Patrick Mazza, of Stormy Weather: 101 Solutions to Global Climate Change. *In the following viewpoint Dauncey argues that America must change its energy policy in order to cut carbon emissions and reduce global warming. The best way to do this, he claims, is to move away from dirty fossil fuels and toward alternative energy sources. Dauncey asserts that renewable energy sources are abundant and nonpolluting, and could supply most of America's energy needs.*

As you read, consider the following questions:

1. According to Dauncey, what problems are associated with the use of natural gas?
2. According to this viewpoint, what is the annual growth of demand for electricity in the United States?
3. What amount of U.S. government subsidies are given to the fossil fuels industry each year, according to the author?

Guy Dauncey, "A Sustainable Energy Plan for the U.S.," *Earth Island Journal*, vol. 18, Fall 2003.

Every morning when we rise, we flick on the lights and various electrical appliances before we drive or cycle off to work, school, or play. Somewhere far away, trucks haul coal into the hoppers of giant power plants. Across the oceans, ships bring us oil, which produces the power we need to run our lives. For most North Americans, the system works just fine. We no longer think about where the energy comes from. If there's an energy shortage, all we need to do is burn more coal, drill more oil, and pump more gas. If only it were so simple.

Troublesome Facts

The rate at which we are discovering new oil will soon fall below the rate at which we are using it. As soon as it does, oil prices will shoot up as demand starts to outstrip supply. There's plenty of coal in the ground, but it's a pernicious fuel. Aside from carbon dioxide, burning coal releases nitrous oxides, sulfur dioxide, and mercury, which contribute to smog, asthma, acid rain, and poisoned lakes and rivers.

The world's climate is responding to the increase in atmospheric CO_2, methane, and nitrogen oxides caused by burning fossil fuels. All three gases trap heat. Before the industrial age, atmospheric CO_2 was around 280 parts per million. Today, it is 373 ppm, the highest it has been for 20 million years. The Arctic summer icepack, normally three meters thick, has dwindled by 40 percent since 1970. At this rate, it could be gone entirely by 2050. Polar bears, which depend on the ice to hunt, will become extinct. Scientists on the Intergovernmental Panel on Climate Change say that we need an immediate 60 percent reduction in emissions to stabilize the climate at a safe level. In our book, *Stormy Weather: 101 Solutions to Global Climate Change*, Patrick Mazza and I call for an 80 percent reduction by 2025.

Natural gas is not a cleaner alternative or a "bridge to the future" as many people would have us believe. Natural gas produces lower CO_2 emissions than coal or oil, but 85 percent of natural gas is methane, some of which escapes during production and distribution. In a sustainable energy plan, reliance on natural gas would be excluded along with coal and oil.

Nuclear power should also be avoided because of the risk of catastrophic accidents. The idea of a bunch of terrorists flying a jet into a nuclear power plant is not comforting; and no one knows how to deal with the radioactive wastes.

How Much Do We Need?

The challenge for a sustainable energy plan is to meet America's reasonable energy needs using energy from the sun, wind, biomass, geothermal, microhydro [small-scale water power], waves, and tides.

The good news is that the transition to a sustainable energy future is well underway. All that is needed is for the kind of support Washington gives to the coal, oil, and gas industries to be given to the sustainable energy industry instead.

So how much energy do we need? Let's crunch some numbers. In the year 2002, the US consumed 97 quadrillion BTUs of primary energy—the energy used to generate electricity, fuel vehicles, heat buildings and run factories. Industry used 38 percent, transport 32 percent, residential buildings 19 percent, and commercial buildings 16 percent. US electrical generating capacity in 2001 was 813 gigawatts; in that year, US power plants produced 3,836 terawatt hours of electricity—52 percent from coal, 21 percent from nuclear, 16 percent from natural gas, 7 percent from hydro, 2 percent from oil, and 1 percent from non-hydro renewables. A terawatt [TW] is 1,000 gigawatts, or a million megawatts (MW).

The Energy Information Administration estimates that demand for electricity is growing by 1.8 percent per year in the US, and will increase to 5,439 TWh by 2020, requiring 1,300 new power plants to be built—more than one a week. This assumes the current "business as usual," profligate North American energy use levels.

What might we do instead? European countries get by on half as much energy per capita and per unit of Gross Domestic Product (GDP). Using today's technologies, buildings, appliances, factories, and vehicles in North America could be twice as efficient. Using tomorrow's technologies, they could be four to ten times as efficient.

Here are some of the policies that could cut our electricity demand by 75 percent by 2020, to 1,360 TWh, without any loss of quality:

- Apply a mandatory one- to four-star energy efficiency rating to appliances, houses, and vehicles, and give big tax credits for the purchase of four-star items. Award annual "achievement" tax credits to the companies that produce the most efficient appliances and technologies.
- Strengthen the national energy code for buildings, and then build on San Francisco's example: make compliance mandatory for all buildings, new and existing. For nonconforming buildings, make the code kick in whenever a building is sold, a lease renewed, or an owner applies for a building permit for work worth more than $10,000.
- Establish a national electricity efficiency tax, or public benefit charge, as several states have done. This increases the price of electricity, but returns all the revenue in energy efficiency incentives.

Transportation Inefficiencies

In 2002, America's vehicles consumed three billion barrels of oil. Four-fifths of that oil could be saved through a combination of smarter travel, greater fuel efficiency, and a switch to sustainably derived hydrogen, bioethanol, and biodiesel.

America Has a Greater Responsibility to Cut Emissions

Carbon dioxide emissions, 1950–2000

Country	Billions of tons	Percent
United States	181.6	32.0
European Union	127.8	22.5
Russia	68.4	12.1
China	57.6	10.2
Japan	31.2	5.5
Ukraine	21.7	3.8
India	15.5	2.7
Canada	14.9	2.6
Poland	14.4	2.5
Kazakhstan	10.1	1.8
South Africa	8.5	1.5
Mexico	7.8	1.4
Australia	7.6	1.3
TOTAL	**567.1**	**99.9**

SOURCE: *Time*, April 23, 2001, pp. 52–53.

First, let's aim for a 25 percent reduction in motor traffic by investing in bicycle trails, mass transit, and telecommuting. We should also use smart-growth planning principles for new settlements, and retrofit America's suburbs to create small village centers where people can work, shop, and relax.

Next, we need to make our vehicles far more efficient. There are cars on the road today that can get 50 mpg. We should upgrade the Corporate Average Fuel Efficiency (CAFE) standard so that new cars are required to increase their efficiency to 45 mpg by 2010, and to 80 mpg by 2025, with an equivalent increase for trucks, buses, and SUVs. Taken together, these policies will create a four-fold reduction in the energy needed for transport.

Fuels for cars, trucks, and planes of the future will be hydrogen, bioethanol, and biodiesel—and carbohydrate oils from sewage and garbage, should a promising technology known as "thermal depolymerization" work out.

America's bioethanol potential comes from harvesting existing agricultural wastes and low-cost cellulose feedstocks; there is already enough to produce 51 billion gallons a year, equivalent to 40 percent of the current gasoline market, according to Oak Ridge National Laboratory estimates. If our vehicles were four times as efficient—easily achievable under more rigorous CAFE standards—bioethanol and biodiesel from agricultural wastes could provide 40 percent of the fuel they'd need.

Clean Electricity

A reasonable goal for sustainable US electricity consumption is 1,360 TWh by 2025, of which 80 percent must come from clean energy. Since hydrogen will be needed for most of our transportation needs, and the cleanest way to obtain hydrogen is by using renewable energy to split water, we should increase the goal to 4,000 TWh.

Can it be done? No problem. The steps below, taken together, could provide the US with 24,000 TWh, six times more than we need if we gain the efficiencies described above. Producing so much extra energy would give us some options among the most cost-effective, environmentally benign routes. By linking many renewable energy sources together through a smart electronic energy network, or distributed grid, we would gain further efficiencies in production and in price.

A recent study by the World Wildlife Fund shows that the lower 48 states have 14,244 TWh of wind energy potential.

The best land areas are North Dakota, Texas, Kansas, and South Dakota, which have a potential of 4,500 TWh, 17 percent more than America's current electricity demand. It's all good news for the farmers, who can form wind-turbine cooperatives and obtain a steady income while farming underneath, as they do in Denmark. The southern and southeastern coastlines also have excellent offshore wind potential, and Alaska has superb on-land and offshore potential. Together, these could produce an additional 4,000 TWh. Around the world, wind power sells at a very competitive 3–6 cents/kWh, and is among the fastest-growing segments of the energy market. And modern turbine design and judicious siting nearly eliminate the well-publicized risk to birds.

There are 39 countries that could meet all of their energy needs from hot underground water. In Britain, a proposal has been floated to drill two miles deep into Cornwall and tap enough geothermal energy to supply the entire British grid. A similar proposal is being explored in the Charleville area of Australia, which could meet Australia's power needs for hundreds of years. In the US, the GeoPowering the West initiative aims to provide 20 percent of the West's power from geothermal energy by 2020. We can also use ground-source geothermal energy to heat homes, offices, and schools, using off-the-shelf heat pumps to extract heat from the year-round temperature differential six feet down. Our estimate of the potential energy generated by US geothermal projects is 190 TWh.

Solar Energy

Every year, the sun pours 220 million TWh of solar energy onto the Earth's surface, 1,864 times the world's entire energy consumption. At current levels of solar photovoltaic (PV) efficiency, and allowing for cloudier conditions in the north, the entire current US electricity demand (3,836 TWh) could be met from 10,000 square miles of PV, an area equivalent to 9 percent of Arizona. America's rooftops could generate 964 TWh (24 percent of our sustainable electricity needs) if solar shingles were used to roof 540 square feet per dwelling. Many open-air car parks could also be covered, providing welcome shade for the vehicles.

What about the argument that photovoltaic cells require more energy to make than they generate? A 1997 study by Siemens (now Shell Solar) showed that the payback for crystalline silicon PV modules varied from two to five years (for sunny and less sunny areas), and was set to improve to one to two years. For amorphous silicon, the payback was one year. For both technologies, most of the energy cost is for the aluminum that holds the PV module. Move to solar shingles, which have no aluminum, and that cost disappears.

The biggest obstacle to PV is cost. Currently at around $3.50 per installed watt, a 3kW system on your roof might cost $24,750. If you include an assumed 5 percent interest rate, it will take 70 years to pay for itself. With mass production, however, the price falls to $1 per watt, and the payback falls to 17 years. When you add the income from the sale of surplus solar energy on a hot summer's afternoon, the payback could fall to 10 years or lower, and your solar shingles become a money-making machine that will save the planet's atmosphere at the same time.

Early computers and cell phones were expensive—now they're cheap. PV production is growing by 35 percent a year. The Japanese electronics company Sharp plans to open a factory in 2005 that will build 500 MW of PV panels each year. The plan is supported by a consistent set of programs from the Japanese government, which plans to install 4,600 MW of solar in Japan by 2010. With the price of solar at $1 a watt, the solar revolution will take off.

For our Sustainable Energy Plan, we will assume that all south-facing sloping roofs can be covered with solar shingles, and we will use 10,000 square miles of other surface areas (chiefly flat commercial and industrial roofs) to collect solar energy. As the technical efficiency of PV increases, the area needed decreases. We estimate the potential solar energy thus generated at 5,000 TWh.

Wind, sun, and geothermal energy take us well over our goal. In addition, we can probably assume another 1,000 TWh from micro-hydro, tidal and wave energy, biomass, and methane gas from landfills. With this much energy, we can afford to close down the nuclear plants and remove many of the dams that block wild rivers. . . .

Government Policies

We need four basic policies to launch a sustainable energy revolution: energy efficiency standards, renewable portfolio standards, carbon taxes, and tax and subsidy shifts. We have already covered the efficiency policies, so we'll move right on.

Renewable portfolio standards (RPS) require that a percentage of a state's electricity must come from renewable resources by a certain date. Fifteen states have enacted RPSs, led by Nevada, which requires that 15 percent of all energy be generated from renewable sources by 2013 (5 percent from solar), and then increases that by 2 percent each subsequent year. A federal RPS could require that 10 percent of all US energy come from renewable sources by 2010, and 80 percent by 2025. The policy will drive investment, and give industry plenty of time to act. We saw a similar process in 1990, when California required that 4 percent of all new vehicles in California be zero emission by 2003, prompting investment in fuel cell companies.

Carbon taxes are taxes on all fuels that release CO_2 emissions, driving up the price of oil, coal, and natural gas relative to non-carbon energy such as solar, wind, and bioethanol—which does release carbon when burned, but recaptures it when the new feedstock is grown on the farm. Carbon rebates would allow people to reduce their overall energy bills by reducing emissions. Businesses that invest in innovations would benefit as the world shifts to non-fossil fuels. New jobs would be generated, far more than those lost by closing the coalmines and capping the oil and gas wells.

The final policy—a *tax and subsidy shift*—would transfer the subsidies, programs, and tax breaks supporting fossil fuels to efficiency measures, renewable energy, and hydrogen. Those subsidies range from $20–$46 billion a year, depending on which estimate you accept. If you include the costs of fossil fuel–related health and environmental damage, the total might reach $228 billion a year.

> *"Generation of electricity from renewables is limited by costs."*

Renewable Energy Is Not Viable

Jerry Taylor and Peter VanDoren

Jerry Taylor is the director of natural resource studies, and Peter VanDoren is the editor of Regulation *magazine, at the Cato Institute. The authors argue in the following viewpoint that renewable sources of energy are uncompetitive with fossil fuels when the federal government does not subsidize them. Moreover, the authors maintain, renewables are touted as a way to address global warming, but global warming has not been proved to be a problem. For these reasons renewables are not likely to be a viable energy source, the authors conclude.*

As you read, consider the following questions:

1. What percentage of total electricity will renewables supply in 2020, as detailed by this viewpoint?
2. According to the authors, what were the estimated yearly costs associated with the Clean Air Act during the 1970s and 1980s?

Jerry Taylor and Peter VanDoren, "Evaluating the Case for Renewable Energy: Is Government Support Warranted?" *Policy Analysis*, January 10, 2002, pp. 2, 5, 7–11.

3. What four types of pollution associated with the burning of fossil fuels are mentioned in this viewpoint?

Ever since the energy crises of the 1970s, the U.S. government has promoted the use of "renewable energies"—primarily wind, solar, biomass (burning wood and plant material for power), and geothermal (tapping the hot steam or rock beneath the earth)—as desirable substitutes for conventional fossil fuels. Renewable energy (which, for the purposes of this paper, does not include nuclear power or hydropower) is widely thought to be not only more environmentally benign than coal or oil but also nearly as attractive economically.

The state and federal campaign to promote the use of renewable energy, however, has not yet significantly affected electricity generation patterns. Since the establishment of the U.S. Department of Energy in 1978, the federal government has spent more than $11 billion to subsidize—via investment tax credits, production credits, accelerated depreciation of capital costs, publicly funded research and development (R&D), and mandatory purchases at avoided cost—wind, solar, biomass, and geothermal power. Yet those fuels account for only a tiny share of the electricity produced.

Advocates of renewable energy continue to insist that it is poised to gain significant market share over the next several years. Although renewable energy is still more expensive than conventional energy, production costs have come down significantly over the past 22 years, and the gap between the cost of conventional and renewable energy has narrowed substantially. And if nations reduce greenhouse gas emissions, environmentalists argue, renewables will become the lowest-cost sources of electricity fuel on the market.

This study examines the economics of renewable energy in the electricity market and the case for government intervention to promote its use. We reach three conclusions:

- Renewable energy is not likely to gain significant market share in the foreseeable future without a significant increase in government subsidies or mandates.
- Rationales for subsidies for renewable energy and other preferences are without sound economic foundation.
- The threat of global warming is speculative, and such warming is not necessarily deleterious from an economic perspective. Even if restrictions on greenhouse gas emissions were necessary, replacing conventional energy sources with renewable energy would be more costly and less efficient than other emission abatement strategies. . . .

Forecasts for Growth

Advocates of renewable energy often use recent trends in the wind industry—a growth rate of nearly 70 percent from 1997 through 2000, for example—as the basis for predictions about future growth potential. But such arguments can be charitably described as boosterism.

The EIA [Energy Information Administration] generates predictions using the National Energy Modeling Systems, a sophisticated computer model of the industry that is used to forecast changes in energy markets. NEMS forecasts are far less optimistic about the near or midterm prospects for renewable energy than are the forecasts of advocates of renewable energy.

Absent significant changes in federal policy, the EIA projects that installed renewable energy capacity (including both direct generation and industrial cogeneration) will increase by 7.5 gigawatts by 2020, giving renewable energy 2.8 percent of net generation in the electricity marketplace and 3.1 percent of retail electricity sales. Combined-cycle turbine plants, fired primarily by natural gas, are expected to account

Next Generation of Electricity from Various Fuels

Fuel	Kilowatt-hours (millions)	Percentage of Total Electricity Generation
Nonrenewables and hydro	3,799,944	97.79
Renewables		
Biomass	39,498	1.04
Waste combustion	24,590	0.65
Geothermal	14,197	0.37
Wind	4,953	0.13
Solar	844	0.02
Total renewables	84,082	2.21

SOURCE: Energy Information Administration, Monthly Energy Review Interactive Data Query System, http://tonto.eia.doe.gov/mer, 2000.

for 92 percent of new capacity over that same period because their costs are expected to be lower than those of other sources of electricity. Even coal-fired electricity is expected to add three times more capacity to the system than renewable-fired electricity generation. To put the projected expansion of renewable energy into perspective, the additional expected power equals the electricity output from 3–4 moderately sized coal or nuclear power plants over the next 20 years.

Of the 5,356 megawatts (MW) of renewable energy generating capacity currently planned through 2020, only 291 MW are being built voluntarily; the rest of the investment is a consequence of state mandates and orders. Thus, government orders, not economic competitiveness, account for even the modest amount of new renewable generating capacity expected over the next two decades. . . .

Real Fossil Fuel Electricity Costs

Generation of electricity from renewables is limited by costs. Advocates of renewable energy know this so they argue that the demand for renewables would rise if conventionally generated electricity were priced to reflect its pollution costs.

The argument that fossil fuel extraction and combustion foul the environment in ways that are incompatible with property rights and markets has some merit. Air and water resources have been treated as a public commons rather than as private property. Advocates of renewable energy argue that consumers of fossil fuels have not had to indemnify anyone for the environmental consequences of their consumption and thus prices for fossil fuels are too low. Consequently, society consumes "too much" fossil fuel.

Although a world of relatively "unpriced" pollution existed prior to 1970 and the enactment of the Clean Air Act amendments, environmental regulation since the 1970s has imposed large costs on firms, particularly new coal-burning utilities, and those costs have been passed on to consumers. So, in a sense, consumers of electricity *have* had to pay a premium for the environmental consequences of the fossil fuels they consume. For example, the costs of compliance with the Clean Air Act through the 1970s and 1980s (the "environmental tax" on fossil fuels) were about $25 billion to $35 billion annually. The relevant question, then, is whether the regulatory cost paid by consumers already covers the environmental "cost" of fossil fuel consumption.

The answer, unfortunately, is not at all clear. The estimates of the economic damage caused by fossil fuel consumption are all over the map. If we accept EPA's [Environmental Protection Agency's] estimates as a reasonable point of analytic departure, however, we find that biomass and coal are somewhat undertaxed relative to their external costs, natural gas is substantially overtaxed, and gasoline is taxed correctly. . . .

Because pollution policies already control emissions and a reasonable interpretation of the evidence suggests that the additional cost of further exposure reduction exceeds the additional health benefits, the economically efficient subsidy for alternative electricity sources is probably zero.

Even if current regulatory costs are insufficiently reflective of true environmental costs, they are not so far off the mark that "getting prices right" would significantly affect consumer decisions about fuels. . . .

Does Global Warming Alter the Conclusion?

Even if the scientific alarmists are correct about the effects of anthropogenic [human-caused] greenhouse gas emissions, it is not clear that the benefits of restricting fossil fuel consumption outweigh the costs. And unless the benefits of "doing something" about global warming outweigh the costs, the efficient greenhouse gas "tax" on coal- or gas-fired electricity is zero.

Accordingly, the case for promoting renewable energy to "do something" about global warming is empirically weak. Moreover, as we discussed earlier, embracing a policy of "doing something" about global warming does not necessarily translate into a policy of subsidizing renewable energy; there are far less costly means of reaching that end.

Do Subsidies for Traditional Fuels Justify Subsidies for Renewables?

The EIA reported that energy subsidies in fiscal year 1999 totaled $4 billion. The oil industry received $312 million, the coal industry received $489 million, and the natural gas industry received $1.2 billion (almost all of which was a tax credit for the production of alternative fuels, primarily gas from tight sands and coalbed methane). Renewable energy was the recipient of $1.1 billion in subsidies in 1999. Subsidies for fossil fuels amount to only 1 percent of total energy purchases and are, according to EIA, "too small to have a significant effect on the overall level of energy prices and consumption in the United States."

R&D [research and development] dollars have not handicapped renewable energy technologies. Over the past 20 years, those technologies have received (in inflation-adjusted 1996 dollars) $24.2 billion in federal R&D subsidies, while nuclear energy has received $20.1 billion and fossil fuels only $15.5 billion. To the extent that nuclear power has received heavy favor from government, the primary victims have been oil, gas, and coal—not renewable energy.

The best way to "level the playing field" is to eliminate subsidies for traditional sources rather than enact new programs for renewables. . . .

Renewable Energy Portfolio Standards

Ten states have adopted renewable energy portfolio standards (RPS), which require that a certain percentage of the state's electricity supply be produced from eligible renewable energy sources. . . .

A "hard" 20 percent RPS [nationwide] would provide the equivalent of a 5 cent per kWh subsidy for renewable-fired electricity, increasing the amount of renewable energy sold on the market from the 135 billion kWh otherwise projected in 2020 to 932 billion kWh, a 690 percent increase. Approximately 57 percent would come from biomass cofired with coal, 30 percent from wind-powered turbines, 11 percent from geothermal facilities, and 2 percent from landfill gas. According to EIA, electricity prices would be 3 percent higher in 2010 and 4 percent higher in 2020 under a hard 20 percent RPS.

In sum, moderate RPS programs accomplish little and aggressive RPS programs would prove quite expensive. Moreover, because the primary beneficiary of those programs would be biomass, which would be mixed with coal in existing coal-

Mike Keefe for "It's the Latest in Hybrid Technology." Reproduced by permission of Cagel Cartoons, Inc.

fired power plants, the environmental benefits would be far less than we might expect. That even aggressive RPS programs are insufficient to significantly expand the market share of wind- and solar-powered electricity underscores just how uncompetitive those technologies are today in the marketplace.

Would Stricter Pollution Controls Increase Renewable Energy Generation?

Regardless of the merits of the claim that conventional sources of electricity are underpriced because of inadequate regulation of pollution emissions, what would happen to the renewable energy industry if pollution rules were tightened on conventional electric power plants?

The main legislative proposals to reduce pollution from power plants address sulfur dioxide (a contributor to "acid rain" and regional haze), nitrogen oxides (a contributor in some regions to summertime urban smog), mercury (a toxic constituent thought by some to harm both human and ecological health), and carbon dioxide (one of the most important greenhouse gases) jointly in coordinated, comprehensive fashion. Those proposals are commonly referred to as "multi-emission" or "4-pollutant" bills. President Bush, after initially calling for adoption of just such a 4-pollutant bill during his campaign for the White House, now supports instead a "3-pollutant" bill addressing sulfur dioxide, nitrogen oxides, and mercury but *not* carbon dioxide.

Reducing emissions of nitrogen oxides and sulfur dioxide by 75 percent below 1997 levels (the most common proposal) would increase electricity prices by only about 1 percent, too little to trigger a shift from coal or natural gas to renewable energy. The EIA notes that, while "scrubbers, selective catalytic reduction, and selective noncatalytic reduction (the most popular technologies for controlling such emissions) can be expensive, they generally are not costly enough to make existing coal-fired plants uneconomical."

Reducing mercury emissions by 90 percent below 1997 levels (the most common proposal) also would not increase renewable energy generation because, according to the EIA, "the [mercury] cap can be met more cost-effectively by retrofitting and switching from coal to natural gas than by switching to more costly renewable energy technologies." In the meantime, combining the proposed mercury regulations with the proposed reductions in emissions of nitrogen oxides and sulfur dioxide (the 3-pollutant approach) would increase electricity prices by 3–4 percent by 2020.

Can Renewable Energy Contribute to a Campaign Against Global Warming?

Perhaps the most common argument for government promotion of renewable energy is that renewable energy can play a significant role in achieving affordable greenhouse gas emission reductions. . . .

For example, if a 7 percent reduction of carbon dioxide emissions below the 1990 baseline were mandated (a 30–42 percent reduction from projected levels), the likely increase in the market share of renewable energy would be 27 percent by 2010 and 32 percent by 2020, giving renewable energy technologies 7 percent of the electricity market in 2020. Biomass (primarily cofired with coal) would achieve the largest market gain, followed by geothermal and wind technologies, respectively.

The costs of such a plan, however, would be significant. Absent an international emissions trading regime, electricity prices would increase by 43 percent in 2010—an average annual "tax" of approximately $218 per household in 2010 and $174 by 2020.

Actually stabilizing greenhouse gas concentrations at present levels would require a 60–80 percent cut in present greenhouse gas emissions and, thus, the nearly complete elimination of fossil fuel consumption because fossil fuel combustion creates about 80 percent of total greenhouse gas emissions. Such an undertaking is simply not conceivable.

VIEWPOINT 3

> *"Increasingly, thoughtful environmentalists see anti-nuclearism as counterproductive."*

Nuclear Energy Can Reduce Pollution

John Ritch

John Ritch is the general director of the World Nuclear Association, an organization that promotes nuclear energy. In this viewpoint Ritch argues that due to the pollution caused by the burning of fossil fuels, more clean nuclear power plants should be built around the world. Ritch sees nuclear energy as being a primary new energy source for the next century because it is environmentally safe. Concerns over radioactive waste are unwarranted, he argues, because such waste can be disposed of easily in underground facilities. Moreover, unlike fossil fuels, producing and using nuclear energy does not pollute, he asserts.

As you read, consider the following questions:

1. According to Ritch, what applications in the next century will use nuclear energy?
2. As cited in this viewpoint, what are the major public concerns over nuclear power?

John Ritch, "The Key to Our Energy Future," *Washington Post*, April 26, 2005, p. A15.

3. In what ways does the author claim that governments can assist nuclear energy development?

In the current debate over the energy bill [which was passed in 2005] one important factor is being all but ignored: A global renaissance in nuclear energy is gaining momentum, and it could have greater implications than any or all of the other proposed methods being discussed for dealing with our energy problems.

Today some 440 civil nuclear reactors, in 30 countries comprising two-thirds of humankind, produce 16 percent of the world's electricity. Under current plans, these nations will construct several hundred more reactors by 2030.

China and India will lead the way, but the expansion will be broad-based. Nuclear power will also extend to new countries as diverse as Poland, Turkey, Indonesia and Vietnam. Meanwhile, nuclear "phaseouts" in countries such as Italy and Germany seem sure to be reversed.

Around the world, there is a new realism about nuclear energy, a recognition of its essential virtue, which is its capacity to deliver power cleanly, safely, reliably and on a massive scale. This thinking is eclipsing old-school anti-nuclear environmentalism.

Increasingly, thoughtful environmentalists see anti-nuclearism as counterproductive. They worry not about the growth of nuclear energy but about the likelihood that it is not growing rapidly enough to produce the clean-energy revolution the world urgently needs.

Carbon fuel emissions—900 tons each second—continue unabated, even as science warns that we are fast reaching a point of irreversible global warming with consequences for sea levels, species extinction, epidemic disease, drought and severe weather events that will disrupt all civilization.

To avert climate catastrophe, greenhouse emissions must be reduced over the next 50 years by 60 percent—even as

Disposal of Nuclear Waste

One commonly cited drawback of nuclear power is that it creates radioactive waste that must be contained for thousands of years.... Of course, radioactive waste can represent a serious hazard if it is not properly maintained, but its small volume allows very high expenditures and great care per unit volume. If all the country's high-level nuclear waste from over three decades of plant operations were collected on a football field, it would be only 9 feet deep. Nuclear power plant wastes have been carefully maintained at the plants for decades without harm to the environment or the public.

Bertram David Wolfe, Issues in Science and Technology, *1996.*

population growth and economic development are combining to double or triple world energy consumption.

Every authoritative energy analysis points to an inescapable imperative: Humankind cannot conceivably achieve a global clean-energy revolution without a rapid expansion of nuclear power to generate electricity, produce hydrogen for tomorrow's vehicles and drive seawater-desalination plants to meet a fast-emerging world water crisis.

Public Concerns over Nuclear Energy

This reality requires a tenfold increase in nuclear energy during the 21st century. Fortunately, advances in technology and practice can facilitate this expansion by meeting legitimate public concerns:

> *Safety.* In the two decades since [the] Chernobyl [nuclear accident] the global nuclear industry has built an impressive safety record that draws on 12,000 reactor-years of practical experience. A network of ac-

tive cooperation on operational safety now links every nuclear power reactor worldwide.

Arms Proliferation. Illicit weapons programs of rogue regimes pose an ever-present risk. But strong, universal safeguards can ensure that civil nuclear facilities do not increase that risk. Security for the environment and against terrorism need not conflict.

Cost. Steady reductions in operational and capital costs have already made nuclear energy highly competitive. Once governments begin to impose a real price on environmental damage—through emissions trading or carbon taxes—the balance will tilt decisively toward nuclear.

Waste. In truth, waste is nuclear power's greatest comparative asset. Unlike carbon emissions, the volume is minimal and can be reliably contained and managed. For a half-century, the civil nuclear industry has safely stored and transported all end products from electricity generation. For long-term storage, a scientific consensus favors deep geological repositories. Governments worldwide must follow the lead of Finland, Sweden, the United States and France by moving to construct such sites.

The scope of the environmental crisis requires that governments accelerate the nuclear renaissance. One essential element will be a comprehensive ... treaty on climate. It must include all major nations and yield a steady, long-term contraction in global emissions. The key is an emissions-trading mechanism that yields efficiency in clean-energy investment and a net flow of investment from North to South. This economic assistance will be the most cost-effective in history if it prevents the globally destructive greenhouse emissions that will otherwise occur in the developing world.

Nuclear Investment

Another key is investment. Full-scale nuclear investment is still impeded by the absence of carbon penalties, the short-term bias of deregulated energy markets and the fact that 21st-century nuclear reactors have not yet achieved economies of scale. Governments must prime the pump using start-up aids such as loan guarantees and tax credits for first-of-a-kind engineering costs.

We need multinational investment, too. Today the major U.N. [United Nations] development institutions reflexively embrace unscientific prejudice while the International Atomic Energy Agency works alone to promote the peaceful uses of nuclear energy. Governments must now direct the World Bank and the U.N. Development and Environment Programs to pursue a clean-energy vision with nuclear power in a central role.

Recently, leading academic institutions in 25 countries formed a partnership called the World Nuclear University to build standards for a globalizing nuclear profession. To support this effort, governments worldwide should marshal their own resources—and we must summon the great philanthropies—to supply a global infusion of scholarship funds for studies in peaceful nuclear science.

Today technology is spurring a growth in world population and energy consumption that jeopardizes the future of our biosphere. Wisely used, modern technology can also be our salvation.

"Contrary to the nuclear industry's propaganda, nuclear power is . . . not green and it is certainly not clean."

Nuclear Energy Will Not Reduce Pollution

Helen Caldicott

Helen Caldicott is a medical doctor and the founder of Physicians for Social Responsibility. She has been nominated for the Nobel Peace Prize. In the following viewpoint Caldicott argues that the costs and dangers associated with nuclear energy far outweigh the benefits. Nuclear energy is not a clean energy option, Caldicott contends, noting that fossil fuels are burned in enriching uranium, and toxic pollution is discharged at nuclear facilities. Caldicott also argues that the disposal of nuclear waste, which presents a serious threat to human health, creates a large environmental and scientific challenge.

As you read, consider the following questions:

1. According to Caldicott, what costs associated with nuclear energy are subsidized by the government?
2. Which pollutants, according to this viewpoint, are emitted during uranium enrichment?

Helen Caldicott, "Outside View: Huge Costs of Nuclear Power," *Houston Chronicle*, May 25, 2005.

3. Which four dangerous radioactive elements produced by nuclear plants are listed by the author?

There is a huge propaganda push by the nuclear industry to justify nuclear power as a panacea for the reduction of global-warming gases.

At present [as of April 2005] there are 442 nuclear reactors in operation around the world. If, as the nuclear industry suggests, nuclear power were to replace fossil fuels on a large scale, it would be necessary to build 2,000 1,000-megawatt reactors. Considering that no new nuclear plant has been ordered in the United States since 1978, this proposal is less than practical. Furthermore, even if we decided today to replace all fossil-fuel-generated electricity with nuclear power, there would only be enough economically viable uranium to fuel the reactors for three to four years.

Costs and Emissions

The true economies of the nuclear industry are never fully accounted for. The cost of uranium enrichment is subsidized by the U.S. government. The true cost of the industry's liability in the case of an accident in the United States is estimated to be $560 billion, but the industry pays $9.1 billion—98 percent of the insurance liability is covered by the federal government. The cost of decommissioning all the existing U.S. nuclear reactors is estimated to be $33 billion. These costs—plus the enormous expense involved in the storage of radioactive waste for a quarter of a million years—are not included in the economic assessments of nuclear electricity.

It is said that nuclear power is emission-free. The truth is very different.

In the United States, where much of the world's uranium is enriched, including Australia's, the enrichment facility at Paducah, Ky., requires the electrical output of two 1,000-

megawatt coal-fired plants, which emit large quantities of carbon dioxide, the gas responsible for 50 percent of global warming.

Also, this enrichment facility and another at Portsmouth, Ohio, release from leaky pipes 93 percent of the chlorofluorocarbon gas emitted yearly in the United States. The production and release of CFC gas is banned internationally by the Montreal Protocol because it is the main culprit responsible for stratospheric ozone depletion. But CFC is also a global warmer, 10,000 to 20,000 times more potent than carbon dioxide.

In fact, the nuclear fuel cycle utilizes large quantities of fossil fuel at all of its stages—the mining and milling of uranium, the construction of the nuclear reactor and cooling towers, robotic decommissioning of the intensely radioactive reactor at the end of its 20- to 40-year operating lifetime, and transportation and long-term storage of massive quantities of radioactive waste.

Radioactive Releases

Contrary to the nuclear industry's propaganda, nuclear power is therefore not green and it is certainly not clean. Nuclear reactors consistently release millions of curies [units of radioactivity] of radioactive isotopes into the air and water each year. These releases are unregulated because the nuclear industry considers these particular radioactive elements to be biologically inconsequential. This is not so.

These unregulated isotopes include the noble gases krypton, xenon and argon, which are fat-soluble and if inhaled by persons living near a nuclear reactor, are absorbed through the lungs, migrating to the fatty tissues of the body, including the abdominal fat pad and upper thighs, near the reproductive organs. These radioactive elements, which emit high-energy gamma radiation, can mutate the genes in the eggs and sperm and cause genetic disease.

High-Level Waste

High-level radioactive waste is a by-product of nuclear-weapons production and commercial reactors. . . . High-level waste will be dangerously radioactive forever—that is, for at least tens of thousands of years. One estimate of their toxicity suggests that less than 1 gallon of the waste would be enough to bring every person in the world to the danger level for radiation exposure if it were evenly distributed. There are now about 100 million gallons in storage at 158 sites in 40 states.

Harvey Blatt, America's Environmental Report Card, *2005.*

Tritium, another biologically significant gas which is also routinely emitted from nuclear reactors, is a radioactive isotope of hydrogen composed of two neutrons and one proton with an atomic weight of 3. The chemical symbol for tritium is H3. When one or both of the hydrogen atoms in water is displaced by tritium the water molecule is then called tritiated water. Tritium is a soft energy beta emitter, more mutagenic than gamma radiation, which incorporates directly into the DNA molecule of the gene. Its half-life is 12.3 years, giving it a biologically active life of 246 years. It passes readily through the skin, lungs and digestive system and is distributed throughout the body.

Problems of Nuclear Waste Storage

The dire subject of massive quantities of radioactive waste accruing at the 442 nuclear reactors across the world is also rarely, if ever, addressed by the nuclear industry. Each typical 1,000-megawatt nuclear reactor manufactures 33 metric tons of thermally hot, intensely radioactive waste per year.

Already more than 80,000 metric tons of highly radioactive waste sits in cooling pools next to the 103 U.S. nuclear power plants, awaiting transportation to a storage facility yet to be found. This dangerous material will be an attractive target for terrorist sabotage as it travels through 39 states on roads and railway lines for the next 25 years.

But the long-term storage of radioactive waste continues to pose a problem. Congress in 1987 chose Yucca Mountain in Nevada, 90 miles northwest of Las Vegas, as a repository for the United States' high-level waste. But Yucca Mountain has subsequently been found to be unsuitable for the long-term storage of high-level waste because it is a volcanic mountain made of permeable pumice stone and it is transected by 32 earthquake faults.

Last week [April 2005] a congressional committee discovered fabricated data about water infiltration and cask corrosion in Yucca Mountain that had been produced by personnel in the U.S. Geological Survey. These startling revelations, according to most experts, have almost disqualified Yucca Mountain as a waste repository, meaning that the United States has nowhere to deposit its expanding nuclear waste inventory.

To make matters worse, a study released last week [April 2005] by the National Academy of Sciences shows that the cooling pools at nuclear reactors, which store 10 to 30 times more radioactive material than that contained in the reactor core, are subject to catastrophic attacks by terrorists, which could unleash an inferno and release massive quantities of deadly radiation—significantly worse than the radiation released by Chernobyl, according to some scientists.

Nuclear Waste and Health Hazards

This vulnerable high-level nuclear waste contained in the cooling pools at 103 nuclear power plants in the United States includes hundreds of radioactive elements that have different biological impacts on the human body, the most important being cancer and genetic diseases.

The incubation time for cancer is five to 50 years following exposure to radiation. It is important to note that children, old people and immuno-compromised individuals are many times more sensitive to the malignant effects of radiation than other people.

I will describe four of the most dangerous elements made in nuclear power plants.

Iodine 131, which was released at the nuclear accidents at Sellafield in Britain, Chernobyl in Ukraine and Three Mile Island in the United States, is radioactive for only six weeks and it bio-concentrates in leafy vegetables and milk. When it enters the human body via the gut and the lung, it migrates to the thyroid gland in the neck, where it can later induce thyroid cancer. In Belarus more than 2,000 children have had their thyroids removed for thyroid cancer, a situation never before recorded in pediatric literature.

Strontium 90 lasts for 600 years. As a calcium analogue, it concentrates in cow and goat milk. It accumulates in the human breast during lactation and in bone, where it can later induce breast cancer, bone cancer and leukemia.

Cesium 137, which also lasts for 600 years, concentrates in the food chain, particularly meat. On entering the human body, it locates in muscle, where it can induce a malignant muscle cancer called a sarcoma.

Plutonium 239, one of the most dangerous elements known to humans, is so toxic that one-millionth of a gram is carcinogenic. More than 440 pounds is made annually in each 1,000-megawatt nuclear power plant.

Plutonium is handled like iron in the body, and is therefore stored in the liver, where it causes liver cancer, and in the bone, where it can induce bone cancer and blood malignancies. On inhalation it causes lung cancer. It also crosses the placenta, where, like the drug thalidomide, it can cause severe congenital deformities.

Plutonium has a predisposition for the testicle, where it can cause testicular cancer and induce genetic diseases in future generations. Plutonium lasts for 500,000 years, living on to induce cancer and genetic diseases in future generations of plants, animals and humans.

Plutonium is also the fuel for nuclear weapons—only 11 pounds is necessary to make a bomb and each reactor makes more than 440 pounds per year. Therefore any country with a nuclear power plant can theoretically manufacture 40 bombs a year.

Nuclear power therefore leaves a toxic legacy to all future generations, because it produces global warming gases, because it is far more expensive than any other form of electricity generation, and because it can trigger proliferation of nuclear weapons.

VIEWPOINT 5

> *"Wind energy is zero-emissions energy, a renewable resource that is one of our last, best hopes for staving off devastating climate change."*

Wind Energy Benefits the Environment

Jim Motavalli

Jim Motavalli is a journalist and editor of E/The Environmental Magazine. *Motavalli is also the author of* Forward Drive: The Race to Build "Clean" Cars for the Future *and* Feeling the Heat: Dispatches from the Frontlines of Climate Change. *Motavalli claims in the following viewpoint that wind energy, which is renewable and creates no carbon emissions, can help address global warming caused by the burning of fossil fuels. Moreover, he asserts, today's wind turbines are much more efficient than windmills of the past, resulting in a greater share of America's energy needs being met by wind energy.*

As you read, consider the following questions:

1. According to Motavalli, what new project could be the world's largest wind farm?

2. Which countries listed in this viewpoint have the most wind turbines installed?
3. In what ways does the author claim that the government can assist wind energy development?

At the base of the Sagamore Bridge, the gateway to Cape Cod, is a nostalgia-inducing fake windmill that looks like it belongs with tulips and wooden shoes in an image of Holland's colorful past. In fact, it's advertising for a Christmas tree store, but its mere presence is an irony as the Cape is convulsed in an epic battle over some very real wind turbines. Cape Wind plans to build the first offshore wind park in the U.S. in Nantucket Sound, just five miles off the coast of some of the most exclusive real estate in America. If the project is built, it will at least temporarily set a record as the largest wind farm in the world, its 130 turbines producing 420 megawatts of electricity. If it is defeated by a well-funded opposition group with some highly placed political allies, it will be a resounding defeat for wind power in the U.S., but possibly just a minor setback for a worldwide renewable energy movement that is filling its sails with the inexhaustible power of the wind.

The Growing Power of Wind

Even as the world experiences ever-more-severe storms and sets new temperature records that are being linked to global warming, we're also setting new records for installed wind energy. The two phenomena might appear to be unrelated, but actually they're closely tied together. Wind energy is zero-emissions energy, a renewable resource that is one of our last best hopes for staving off devastating climate change. Wind energy has grown 28 percent annually over the last five years, and the so-called "installed capacity" (the generating power of working wind turbines) doubles every three years: It is the fastest-growing energy source in the world. Some 6,000 megawatts of wind capacity—enough to power 1.5 million homes—are added annually.

The old-fashioned windmills that once pumped water for local farmers have been replaced with high-technology, high-efficiency industrial-grade turbines. The General Electric turbines scheduled to be installed by Cape Wind (resulting from GE's purchase of Enron's wind assets at fire-sale prices) offer a whopping 3.6 megawatts each, are 40 stories tall on thin towers, and boast three prop-like blades the length of two jumbo jets.

As *Business 2.0* reports, "Since 1985, the electric generating capacity of a typical windmill has gone from about 100 kilowatts of constant power to 1.5 megawatts, with a corresponding reduction in cost from 12 cents per kilowatt-hour to less than five cents." Because of federal tax credits (recently renewed until the end of 2005), the real cost of wind power is getting close to such perennials as nuclear, coal and natural gas, which explains the interest of big profit-oriented companies like GE. In 2001, 6,500 megawatts of new wind-generating capacity were installed worldwide, and by 2003 the world had 39,000 megawatts of installed wind power. . . .

A Bright Future . . . with Clouds

The U.S. (6,374 megawatts at the end of 2003) and Europe dominate the development and installation of wind power. Large-scale wind farms both on- and off-shore, can now be found from Denmark to New Zealand. Europe has more than 28,000 installed megawatts of wind power (70 percent of world capacity). World wind leaders include Germany, the U.S., Spain, Denmark and India, each with more than 2,000 megawatts. Germany is in the lead, with 14,609 megawatts installed by the end of 2003. The wind energy industry in Germany employs 35,000 people and supplies 3.5 percent of the nation's electricity. Denmark has the world's highest proportion of electricity generated by wind, more than 20 percent. The Danish Wind Energy Association would like to see that ratcheted up to 35 percent wind power by 2015.

In the U.S. (which gets less than one percent of its energy from wind) the industry rebounded somewhat in the late 1990s. There are now clusters of wind turbines in Texas and Colorado, as well as newly updated sites in California. According to the American Wind Energy Association (AWEA), there are now wind energy products in almost every state west of the Mississippi, and in many Northeastern states. California leads with more than 2,042 megawatts of installed wind energy, followed by Texas, which experienced 500 percent wind growth in 2001 and now has 1,293 megawatts. AWEA explains that one megawatt of wind capacity is enough to supply 240 to 300 average American homes, and California's wind power alone can save the energy equivalent of 4.8 million barrels of oil per year.

AWEA says the U.S. wind industry will install up to 3,000 megawatts of new capacity by 2009. If that proves true, the U.S. will have nearly 10,000 megawatts of wind power, enough to power three million homes. The economics of wind are looking increasingly good. The cost of generating a kilowatt-hour of electricity from wind power has dropped from $1 in 1978 to five cents in 1998, and is expected to drop even further, to 2.5 cents. Wind turbines themselves have dropped in installed cost to $800 per kilowatt. Although, according to the *Financial Times*, wind power is still twice as expensive as generation from a modern oil-fired plant, federal subsidies and tax benefits available in many countries level the playing field.

Government Help

One of the biggest hindrances to even greater wind installation in the U.S. is the on-again, off-again nature of the federal wind energy production tax credit (PTC). Introduced as part of the Energy Policy Act of 1992, PTC granted 1.5 cents per kilowatt-hour (since adjusted for inflation) for the first 10

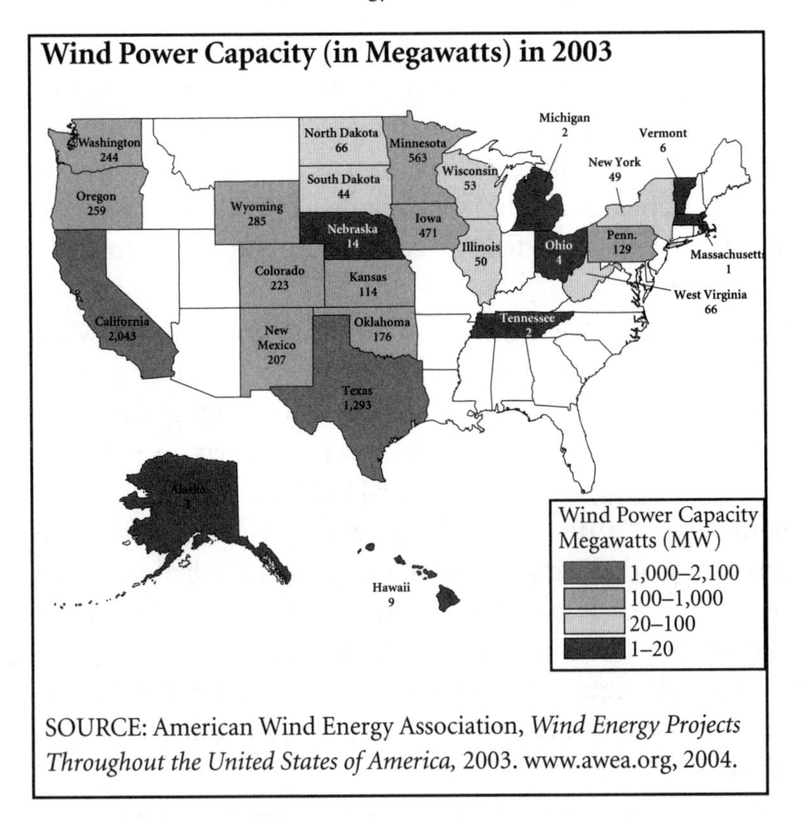

Wind Power Capacity (in Megawatts) in 2003

SOURCE: American Wind Energy Association, *Wind Energy Projects Throughout the United States of America,* 2003. www.awea.org, 2004.

years of operation to wind plants brought on line before the end of June 1999. A succession of short-term renewals and expirations of PTC led to three boom-and-bust cycles (the most recent a boom in 2003 and a bust in 2004) in wind power installation. Its current extension to the end of 2005 may see some wind projects struggling to meet the PTC requirements before the credit expires once again.

The U.S. could go further, and states with big wind resources would reap major rewards. If Congress were to establish a 20 percent national renewable energy standard by 2020 (requiring utilities to sell a fifth of their energy from sustainable sources), the Union of Concerned Scientists reports, wind-rich North Dakota could gain $1.4 billion in new investment from wind and other renewables. North Dakota consumers would save $363 million in lower electricity bills annually if the standard were combined with improvements in energy efficiency. The environment would also benefit with a 28 percent reduction in carbon dioxide emissions from the plains states. A watered-down version of this "renewables portfolio standard" (RPS) was included in the 2002 and 2003 versions of the failed federal energy bill, but failed to make the final cut.

Just such an RPS, on the state level, was enacted when George W. Bush was governor of Texas, and led that state to its pre-eminent status as the number two wind generator in the U.S. Governor George Pataki recently issued an executive order establishing such an RPS for New York State: 20 percent renewables by 2010. New York currently gets 17 percent of its electricity from renewable sources, principally hydro power. The 2004 elections may have been terrible news for the environment, but one bright spot was the passage of a Colorado RPS that will require the state to buy 10 percent of its energy from renewable sources by 2015. Seventeen states have now enacted RPS rules.

AWEA thinks that, with a favorable political climate, the U.S. could have 100,000 megawatts of installed wind power by 2013, with a full potential of 600,000 megawatts. The group points out that wind power could offset a projected three to four billion cubic feet per day natural gas supply shortage in the U.S.

New Wind Projects

Even in the absence of a lucrative production tax credit, wind projects are moving forward. Current projects include construction of the world's third-largest wind farm, with 136 turbines and 204 megawatts capacity, in New Mexico as part of the utility-run New Mexico Wind Energy Center. FPL Energy is also installing 162 megawatts of 1.8-megawatt Danish-made Vestas turbines in Solano County, California for the High Winds project. New England can boast of Green Mountain

Power's project in Searsburg, Vermont, which was completed in 1997 and features 11 turbines generating six megawatts.

Other projects are underway in Oklahoma and South Dakota, on the Rosebud Sioux reservation. Tex Hall of the National Congress of American Indians observes that "tribes here [in the Great Plains] have many thousands of megawatts of potential wind power blowing across our reservation lands.... Tribes need access to the federal grid to bring our value-added electricity to market throughout our region and beyond."

VIEWPOINT 6

> *"Wind energy's environmental benefits are usually overstated, while its significant environmental harms are often ignored."*

Wind Energy Does Not Benefit the Environment

H. Sterling Burnett

H. Sterling Burnett is a senior fellow at the National Center for Policy Analysis, a pro-business think tank. Burnett argues in the following viewpoint that when wind energy is not supported by government subsidies, its costs make it uncompetitive in the free market. He also claims that wind energy is unreliable and that wind farms do not necessarily reduce pollution because they produce only intermittent energy and thus must be backed up by dirty fossil fuel power plants. Moreover, wind energy requires large amounts of land, which spoils the beauty of nature, and turbines kill thousands of birds each year, he asserts.

As you read, consider the following questions:

1. According to Burnett, in what weather conditions do wind turbines fail to produce?

H. Sterling Burnett, "Wind Power: Red Not Green," *Brief Analysis*, February 23, 2004, pp. 1–2.

2. What size "footprints" do various types of energy plants require, as detailed in this viewpoint?
3. What tolls on the environment, according to the author, does maintenance of wind farms take?

Environmentalists have long argued that renewable energy sources (such as wind, solar, and geothermal power, and the burning of biomass), are preferable to fossil fuels (oil, natural gas and coal). Historically, fossil fuels have been relatively abundant and significantly less costly; however, in recent years the price of alternative energies, particularly wind power, has fallen. Under certain conditions, wind power has become cost competitive with conventional fossil fuel energy. In addition, alternative energy advocates claim that burning fossil fuels pollutes the air and emits greenhouse gases that many people argue are causing potentially catastrophic global warming. Renewable energy promoters claim that wind power is cheap, safe and "green." These claims are untrue.

Wind Power Is on the Rise

The price of wind-generated energy fell more steeply than any other energy source over the past 30 years. Indeed, the cost of wind power fell from approximately 25 cents per kilowatt hour (kwh) in the early 1980s to between 5 cents and 7 cents per kwh (adjusting for inflation) currently in prime wind farm areas. Wind advocates argue that a new generation of turbines will bring the cost down below 5 cents per kwh—which is competitive with conventional fossil fuels for electricity generation.

Wind power, currently less than 1 percent of the U.S. power supply, could double its share within 10 years. The American Wind Energy Association has optimistically projected that wind power could provide as much as 6 percent of the nation's energy by 2020.

Wind Power Is in the Red

While the price of wind power has indeed fallen, it still costs more than spot market electric power (3.5 to 4 cents kwh). Furthermore, the price gap between wind and conventional power production is actually greater, since the federal government subsidizes wind power through a production tax credit of 1.8 cents per kwh. Wind power plants also receive accelerated depreciation, allowing owners to write off their costs in five years rather than the usual 20. These subsidies, along with several states' legal requirements that utilities provide some energy from cleaner power sources, account for most and perhaps all of the recent growth in wind power.

Thus, when the 1.8 cent kwh tax credit lapsed in 2003, new wind power projects suddenly became uncompetitive. As a result:

- California's Clipper Windpower abandoned already approved plans to build 67 windmills in Maryland.
- As of January 8, 2004, orders for wind towers from the builder Beaird Industries ground to a halt, costing the company 200 jobs.
- Vestas Wind Technologies shelved plans to build a manufacturing plant in Portland, Ore.
- More than 1,000 megawatts of wind power that would have been added in 2004 will not occur due to the expiration of the tax credit, according to the American Wind Energy Association.

Wind Power Equals Blight

Wind power's environmental benefits are usually overstated, while its significant environmental harms are often ignored.

Despite industry claims, promised air quality improvements have failed to materialize. Because wind is an intermittent resource, wind farms must rely on conventional power

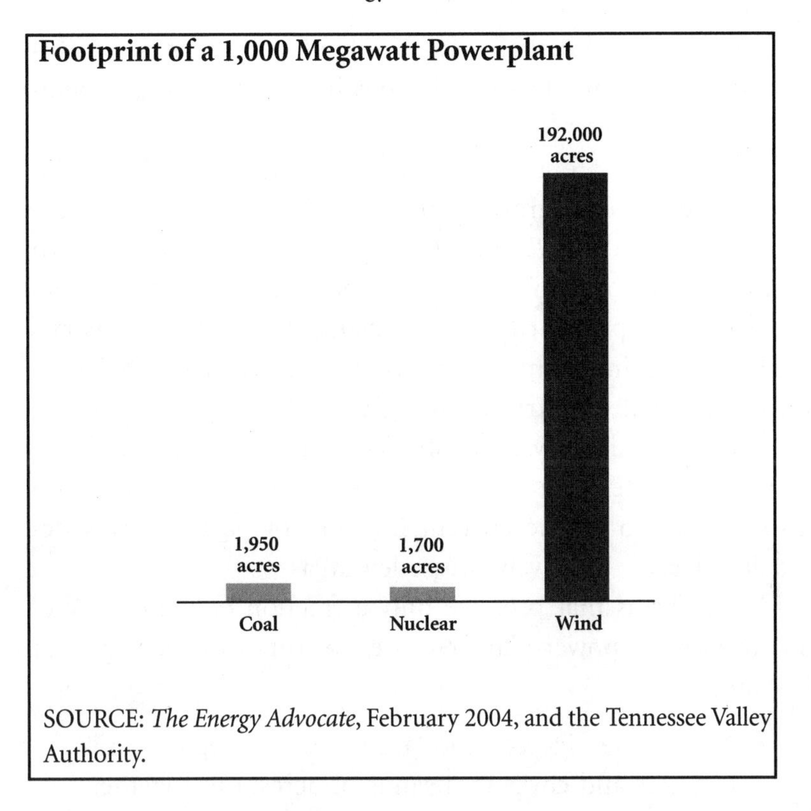

SOURCE: *The Energy Advocate*, February 2004, and the Tennessee Valley Authority.

plants to back up their supply. Wind farms generate power only when the wind is blowing within a certain range of speed. When there is too little wind, the towers don't generate power; but when the wind is too strong, they must be shut down for fear of being blown down. And even when they function properly, wind farms' average output is less than 30 percent of their theoretical capacity.

Bringing a conventional power plant on line to supply power is not as simple as turning on a switch; thus most of the fossil fuel power stations required to supplement wind turbines are not "redundant," but must run continuously, even if at reduced levels. When combined with the CO_2 emitted and pollutants released in the manufacture and maintenance of wind towers and their associated infrastructure, substituting wind power for fossil fuels does little to reduce air pollution.

Wind farms are also land-intensive and unsightly. In Europe, wind power is growing at an even faster rate than in the United States. *Wind Power Monthly*, the British magazine for wind industry enthusiasts, has reportedly recognized that wind power's popularity is decreasing due to the industry's portrayal of wind farms as "parks" in order to trick their way into unspoiled countryside in "green" disguise. Wind farms are more like highways, industrial buildings, railways and factory farms. Often, the most favorable locations for wind farms also happen to be the current location of particularly spectacular views in relatively unspoiled areas.

Wind farms that produce only a fraction of the energy of a conventional power plant require 100 times the acreage. For instance:

- Two of the biggest wind "farms" in Europe have 159 turbines and cover thousands of acres; but together they take a year to produce less than four days' output from a single 2,000 MW (million watt) conventional power station—which uses one percent as much space.
- A proposed wind farm off the Massachusetts coast would produce only 450 MW of power but require 130 towers and more than 24 square miles of ocean.
- A comparison of "footprints" is telling: to produce 1,000 MW of power, a wind farm would require approximately 192,000 acres, or 300 square miles; a nuclear plant needs less than 1,700 acres, or 2.65 square miles (within its security perimeter fence); and a coal powered plant takes up about 1,950 acres, 3.05 square miles.

In addition, regular wind-tower maintenance requires miles of paved roads, increasing runoff and reducing soil moisture absorption. The damage to wildlife habitat is often greater than that from technologies associated with conventional fossil fuels.

Wind Power Versus Birds and Bats

The most publicized environmental harm caused by wind power may be its effects on birds and bats. Wind farms must be located where the wind blows fairly constantly. Unfortunately, such locations are often prime travel routes for migratory birds, including protected species like Bald Eagles and Golden Eagles. The Sierra Club labeled wind towers "the Cuisinarts of the air." Why?

- Scientists estimate as many as 44,000 birds have been killed over the past two decades by wind turbines in the Altamont Pass, east of San Francisco.
- The victims include kestrels and red-tailed hawks, and—since the area is home to the largest resident population of golden eagles in the lower 48 states—an average of 50 golden eagles each year.
- One study shows even more problems, explaining, "Wind farms have been documented to act as both bait and executioner—rodents taking shelter at the base of turbines multiply with the protection from raptors, while in turn their greater numbers attract more raptors to the farm."
- Further, at least 400 migrating bats, including red bats, eastern pipistrelles, hoary bats, and possibly endangered Indiana bats, were killed at a 44-turbine wind farm in West Virginia in 2003.

Bird kill is also a problem in other countries. At Terifa in Spain, the site of 269 wind turbines, thousands of birds from more than 13 protected species have been killed.

Lawsuits may prevent the expansion of wind farms in West Virginia and California, and the construction of wind farms off the New England coast. Indeed, the lead scientist for the Audubon Society called for a moratorium on new wind power development in bird-sensitive areas—which include most of the suitable sites for construction.

Conclusion

Wind power is expensive, doesn't deliver the environmental benefits it promises and imposes substantial environmental costs. Accordingly, it does not merit continued government promotion or funding.

VIEWPOINT 

"It is possible to reduce carbon emissions while making money in the process."

America Should Reduce Its Use of Fossil Fuels

Lester R. Brown

Lester R. Brown, president of the Earth Policy Institute, is the author of Eco-Economy: Building an Economy for the Earth *and* Plan B: Rescuing a Planet Under Stress and a Civilization in Trouble, *from which the following viewpoint has been taken. In it Brown argues that the emissions reductions required by the international Kyoto Protocol are easily achievable by governments. Brown believes that reducing carbon emissions is both necessary to protect the environment and economically feasible. To reduce emissions he recommends increasing energy efficiency and moving toward renewable energy sources. To support his argument Brown cites examples of corporations that have earned profits while significantly lowering carbon emissions.*

As you read, consider the following questions:

1. According to this viewpoint, by how much must nations reduce carbon dioxide from 1990 levels to stabilize the atmosphere?

Lester R. Brown, *Plan B: Rescuing a Planet under Stress and a Civilization in Trouble*, New York, NY: W.W. Norton and Company, 2003.

2. How could the United States reduce the need for new power plants, according to Brown?
3. Which corporations does the author cite as examples of making profits while reducing carbon emissions?

When the Kyoto Protocol [an international emissions treaty] was negotiated in 1997, the proposed 5-percent reduction in carbon emissions from 1990 levels in industrial countries by 2012 seemed like an ambitious goal. Now it is seen by more and more people as being out of date. Even before the treaty has entered into force, many of the countries committed to carrying it out have discovered that they can do even better.

National governments, local governments, corporations, and environmental groups are coming up with ambitious plans to cut carbon emissions. Prominent among these is a plan developed by the British government to reduce carbon emissions 60 percent by 2050, the amount that scientists deem necessary to stabilize atmospheric carbon dioxide (CO_2) levels. Building on this, Prime Minister Tony Blair and Sweden's Prime Minister Göran Persson are jointly urging the European Union to adopt the 60-percent goal.

A plan developed for Canada by the David Suzuki Foundation and the Climate Action Network would halve carbon emissions by 2030 and would do it only with investments in energy efficiency that are profitable. And in early April 2003, the World Wildlife Fund released a peer-reviewed analysis by a team of scientists that proposed reducing carbon emissions from U.S. electric power generation 60 percent by 2020. This proposal centers on a shift to more energy-efficient power generation equipment, the use of more-efficient household appliances and industrial motors and other equipment, and in some situations a shift from coal to natural gas. If implemented, it would result in national savings averaging $20 billion a year from now until 2020.

In Canada's most populous province, an environmental group—the Ontario Clear Air Alliance—has devised a plan to phase out the province's five coal-fired power plants, the first one in 2005 and the last one by 2015. The plan is supported by all three major political parties. Jack Gibbons, director of the Alliance, says of coal burning, "It's a nineteenth century fuel that has no place in twenty-first century Ontario."

Germany, which has set the pace for reducing carbon emissions among industrial countries, is now talking about lowering its emissions by 40 percent by 2020. And this is a country that is already far more energy-efficient than the United States. Contrasting goals for cutting carbon emissions in Germany and the United States are due to a lack of leadership in the latter—not a lack of technology.

U.S.-based Interface, the world's largest manufacturer of industrial carpeting, cut carbon emissions in its Canadian affiliate during the 1990s by two thirds from the peak. It did so by examining every facet of its business—from electricity consumption to trucking procedures. The company has saved more than $400,000 a year in energy expenditures. CEO Ray Anderson says, "Interface Canada has reduced greenhouse gas emissions by 64 percent from the peak, and made money in the process, in no small measure because our customers support environmental responsibility." The Canadian plan to cut carbon emissions in half by 2030 was inspired by the profitability of the Interface initiative.

Although stabilizing atmospheric CO_2 levels is a staggering challenge, it is entirely doable. Detailed studies by governments and by various environmental groups are beginning to reveal the potential for reducing carbon emissions while saving money in the process. With advances in wind turbine design and the evolution of the fuel cell, we now have the basic technologies needed to shift quickly from a carbon-based to a hydrogen-based energy economy. Cutting world carbon emissions in half by 2015 is entirely within range. Ambitious though this might seem, it is commensurate with the threat that climate change poses.

Raising Energy Productivity

The enormous potential for raising energy productivity becomes clear in comparisons among countries. Some countries in Europe have essentially the same living standard as the United States yet use scarcely half as much energy per person. But even the countries that use energy most efficiently are not close to realizing the full potential for doing so.

In April 2001, the Bush administration released a new energy plan and called for construction of 1,300 new power plants by 2020. Bill Prindle of the Washington-based Alliance to Save Energy responded by pointing out how the country could eliminate the need for those plants and save money in the process. He ticked off several steps that would reduce the demand for electricity: Improving efficiency standards for household appliances would eliminate the need for 127 power plants. More stringent residential air conditioner efficiency standards would eliminate 43 power plants. Raising commercial air conditioner standards would eliminate the need for 50 plants. Using tax credits and energy codes to improve the efficiency of new buildings would save another 170 plants. Similar steps to raise the energy efficiency of existing buildings would save 210 plants. These five measures alone from the list suggested by Prindle would not only eliminate the need for 600 power plants, they would save money too.

Of course, each country will have to fashion its own plan for raising energy productivity. Nevertheless, there are a number of common components. Some are quite simple but highly effective, such as banning the use of nonrefillable beverage containers, eliminating the use of incandescent light bulbs, doubling the fuel efficiency of automobiles, and redesigning urban transport systems to raise efficiency and increase mobility.

Snubbing Kyoto

Next Wednesday [February 2005], in the enormous glass-paneled European Union Parliament building in Brussels, hundreds of men and women will gather to mark the start of a new era. . . .

The treaty is the Kyoto Protocol [to reduce carbon emissions], a collective response to the greatest security crisis in the world—global warming.

But one country will not be celebrating. The United States. Even though almost all European countries are on board, and even though Russia is on board and even though China is on board, the United States, in an act of supreme irresponsibility, is standing on the platform watching the train leave the station. (The only other industrialized nations that have failed to join the protocol are Monaco and Australia.)

This is particularly egregious when you consider that the United States would be by far the most significant participant. That's because it is the single biggest polluter on the planet, accounting for about one-quarter of the world's greenhouse gases.

Laurie David, Los Angeles Times, *February 11, 2005.*

Simple Solutions

We know that it is possible to ban the use of nonrefillable beverage containers because Canada's Prince Edward Island has already done so. And Finland has a stiff tax on nonrefillables that has led to 98-percent container reuse for soft drinks. These actions reduce energy use, water use, and garbage generation. A refillable glass bottle used over and over again requires about 10 percent as much energy per use as an aluminum can, even if the can is recycled. Cleaning, sterilizing, and relabeling a used bottle requires little energy, but recycling aluminum, which has a melting point of 660 degrees Celsius (1220 degrees Fahrenheit), is an energy-intensive process. Banning nonrefillables is a win-win policy initiative because it cuts both energy use and the flow of garbage.

Another simple step is to replace all incandescent light bulbs with compact fluorescent bulbs (CFLs), which use only one third as much electricity and last 10 times as long. In the United States, where 20 percent of all electricity is used for lighting, if each household replaced commonly used incandescents with compact fluorescents, electricity for lighting would be cut in half. The combination of lasting longer and using less electricity greatly outweighs the higher costs of the CFLs, yielding a risk-free return of some 25–40 percent a year. Worldwide, replacing incandescent light bulbs with CFLs would save enough electricity to close hundreds of coal-fired power plants, and it could be accomplished easily within three years if we decided to do it.

A third obvious area for raising energy efficiency is automobiles. In the United States, for example, if all motorists were to shift from their current vehicles with internal combustion engines to cars with hybrid engines, like the Toyota Prius or the Honda Insight, gasoline use could be cut in half. Sales of hybrid cars, introduced into the U.S. market in 1999, reached an estimated 46,000 in 2003. . . . Higher gasoline prices and a tax deduction of up to $2,000 for purchasing a low-emission vehicle are boosting sales. With U.S. auto manufacturers coming onto the market on a major scale soon, hybrid vehicle sales are projected to reach 1 million in 2007.

Redesigning Urban Transport

A somewhat more complex way to raise energy productivity is to redesign urban transport systems. Most systems, now automobile-centered, are highly inefficient, with the majority of cars carrying only the driver. Replacing this with a more diverse system that would include a well-developed light-rail system complemented with buses as needed and that was bicycle- and pedestrian-friendly could increase mobility, reduce air pollution, and provide exercise. This is a win-win-win situation. Mobility would be greater, the air would be cleaner, and it would be easier to exercise. Fewer automobiles would mean that parking lots could be converted into parks, creating more civilized cities.

In order to begin shifting the mix away from automobiles, some cities now charge cars entering the city. Pioneered by Singapore many years ago, this approach is now being used in Oslo and Melbourne. And in February 2003, London introduced a similar system to combat congestion as well as pollution, charging $8 for any vehicle entering the central city during the working day. This immediately reduced traffic congestion by 24 percent. . . .

Renewable Energy

Shifting to renewable sources of energy, such as wind power, opens up vast new opportunities for lowering fossil fuel dependence. Wind offers a powerful alternative to fossil fuels—a way of dramatically cutting carbon emissions. Wind energy is abundant, inexhaustible, cheap, widely distributed, climate-benign, and clean—which is why it has been the world's fastest-growing energy source over the last decade. . . .

As wind electric generation expands, the first step would be to back out of coal-fired power plants, either closing them or using them as a backup for wind. Coal-fired plants are the most climate-disruptive energy source simply because coal is almost pure carbon. Coal burning is also the principal source of the mercury deposits that contaminate freshwater lakes and streams. The prevalence of mercury-contaminated fish has led 44 state governments in the United States to issue warnings to consumers to limit or avoid eating fish because of the effect of mercury on the central nervous system. The Centers for Disease Control and Prevention issued a warning in 2001 indicating that an estimated 375,000 babies born each year in the United States are at risk of impaired mental development and learning disabilities because of exposure to mercury.

While it is fashionable for some industries and industry groups to complain that reducing carbon emissions, even by the very modest 5 percent required by the Kyoto Protocol, would be costly and a burden on the economy, the reality is that reducing carbon emissions is one of the most profitable investments that many companies can make. Study after study has concluded that it is possible to reduce carbon emissions while making money in the process.

The experience of individual companies confirms this. DuPont, one of the world's largest chemical manufacturers, has already cut its greenhouse gas emissions from their 1990 level by 65 percent. In an annual report, CEO Chad Holliday, Jr., proudly reports savings of $1.5 billion in energy efficiency gains from 1990 to 2002.

> *"The facts have always made it clear [the Kyoto protocol to reduce global warming] would be outrageously costly and completely ineffective."*

America Should Not Reduce Its Use of Fossil Fuels

S. Fred Singer

S. Fred Singer is president of the Science and Environmental Policy Project and a professor emeritus of environmental sciences at the University of Virginia. In the following viewpoint Singer argues that the Kyoto Protocol, the international treaty to reduce carbon emissions, would be economically costly for the United States and would not significantly reduce global warming. Singer critiques the science upon which the protocol is based, claiming that there is no solid evidence supporting the theory of global warming. Singer also claims that mild global warming would be good for the world economy.

As you read, consider the following questions:

1. According to this viewpoint, what is the basic requirement of the Kyoto Protocol?
2. Why does the author dispute the "scientific consensus" of the third IPCC?

S. Fred Singer, "Requiem for the Kyoto Protocol," The Heartland Institute, May 1, 2004. Reproduced by permission.

3. According to Singer, why is carbon dioxide beneficial?

It may not be a household word, but by now the Kyoto Protocol has become a well-known political slogan. President George W. Bush has called it "fundamentally flawed," while some environmentalists in America and Europe have said it is essential for saving the Earth's climate and the future of humanity itself.

The Kyoto Protocol is a treaty intended to ration the use of energy to address the concerns of those who believe we face a global warming catastrophe. These worriers include not only environmental groups and anti-capitalist radicals, but also a surprising number of mainstream technocrats throughout the West.

But the facts have always made it clear Kyoto would be outrageously costly and completely ineffective as designed, and it would not noticeably influence the climate. More importantly, in light of recent developments, the treaty is essentially defunct. Now may be the ideal moment to reexamine the origins and shortcomings of the Kyoto Protocol, and to learn its lessons before future global warming treaties repeat its mistakes.

A Treaty on Shaky Ground

The Kyoto Protocol, adopted in 1997, insists on lowering global greenhouse gas emissions in the hope of reaching stabilization at some level, preferably one that is not too high. The basic requirement of the protocol is that industrialized nations (and only industrialized nations) reduce emissions of greenhouse gases to a level 5 percent below emissions in 1990 by the period 2008–2012.

But this requirement does nothing to stabilize the atmospheric concentration of greenhouse gases. At best, Kyoto would merely slow somewhat the rate of rise, which by the year 2020 will be largely determined by emissions from major developing countries like China, India, Brazil, and Mexico—none of which is covered by the accord.

The protocol's main emphasis is on carbon dioxide produced by burning fossil fuels. By contrast, the powerful greenhouse gas methane is barely mentioned—perhaps because its main sources, while human-related, are "natural": rice agriculture and cattle-raising. The protocol does not mention other factors that affect the climate, such as sulfate aerosols from coal-fired power plants, soot from diesel engines, and smoke from the burning of biomass (mostly in developing countries).

The Kyoto Protocol, therefore, would have practically no impact on global temperatures. Even if scrupulously adhered to, it would reduce the calculated temperature rise by 0.05 degrees Celsius at most—an amount so insignificant it can hardly be measured.

When confronted with that little-publicized fact, supporters of the protocol admit Kyoto is intended only as a first step, and that greenhouse gases will someday have to be further reduced by between 60 and 80 percent of 1990 emission levels. This fact, too, has not been much publicized by Kyoto's supporters, and with good reason: Such drastic reductions would cripple the global economy.

Questionable Science

To understand the flaws of the Kyoto Protocol, it is necessary to look first at the climate science that allegedly provides a rationale for its provisions.

The groundwork for Kyoto was laid by a series of studies conducted by a United Nations–appointed group, the Intergovernmental Panel on Climate Change (IPCC). Its first report was issued in 1990 and suggested that if the concentration of greenhouse gases were to double, a global warming of between 1.5 and 4.5 degrees Celsius would follow. Those numbers were based on crude climate models whose validity had never been tested by observations—and even today, there remains no validation for the climate models that are at the heart of most claims of climate catastrophe. . . .

Despite the paucity of proof for past climate claims, the third IPCC report said "new evidence" makes it likely "most of the warming observed over the last 50 years" comes from the human production of greenhouse gases. This "new evidence" is based on a single analysis of "proxy" data (that is, data that do not come from thermometers but rather from sources like tree rings, ice cores, corals, and ocean and lake sediments) showing the twentieth century to be the warmest in the past thousand years. Not only does this analysis conflict with other published analyses of proxy data, but it was also exploded in a re-analysis published in 2003, which showed the IPCC claim was the result of a gross mishandling of the underlying data. If the dispute is settled in favor of the re-analysis—as seems likely—the IPCC claim of a "human influence on global climate" will be severely damaged.

The response of global warming theorists to these contrary findings has been twofold: One strategy has been to attack and attempt to discredit both the satellite data and the re-analysis of the proxy data; the other has been simply to ignore any contrary evidence. They make repeated references to the "warming of the past 25 years" but never mention the total lack of warming evidenced in both satellite and balloon observations.

To ensure the disparities do not get publicized, environmental lobbying groups (and their allies in politics and the media) generally refer to the science as "settled." They refer to the "scientific consensus" of the 2,000 or so scientists connected to the IPCC, even though probably no more than 100 of those are true climate specialists; many are actually social scientists and government functionaries, and the list includes some skeptics of global warming who have expressed doubts about the IPCC's conclusions.

Kyoto Would Harm the U.S. Economy

President Bush is right to walk away from the Kyoto Protocol. It is a flawed agreement for addressing the issue of global temperature changes and their impact on the environment. Considerable uncertainty remains about the science of climate change and mankind's contribution to it. As John Christy, a professor of atmospheric science at the University of Alabama in Huntsville, recently stated, "climate models are really in the infancy of being able to predict the future." Therefore, any agreement based on these models is based on speculation, not fact.

Furthermore, any agreement that allows the developing countries to continue emitting greenhouse gases would in effect negate the efforts of those countries that are trying to reduce them. It would drastically increase the cost of gasoline, electricity, and fuel oil for Americans and cause significant harm to the U.S. economy.

Charli E. Coon,
"Why President Bush Is Right to Abandon the Kyoto Protocol,"
Heritage Foundation, 2001. www.heritage.org.

Dead on Arrival

Even before the protocol was adopted, it became clear it would include strict targets and tight timetables for reducing emissions in the industrialized world, with pernicious economic consequences for the United States.

In response, the Senate preemptively and unanimously passed the Byrd-Hagel Resolution in June 1997, which expressed the body's opposition to any attempt to impose strictures that would exempt developing nations and "result in serious harm to the economy of the United States." (The United States would have had to reduce greenhouse gases to a level 7 percent lower than they were in 1990—which by 2012 would amount to a cut of roughly 40 percent.)

And so, even though the Kyoto Protocol was adopted in December 1997 and the Clinton administration signed onto it in 1998, the White House never submitted it to the Senate for ratification, knowing it would be dead on arrival.

Even without American accession to the protocol, Kyoto-related meetings continued: in Buenos Aires in 1998, in Bonn in 1999, and finally, in The Hague in 2000. These annual two-week conferences came to involve some 180 national delegations, with many smaller committee meetings in between....

The sessions in The Hague were highly dramatic, and the conference had to be adjourned without an agreement. Had Europe compromised and permitted emission trading,[1] as requested by the U.S., an agreement might have been possible. But western European nations, especially France, wanted to see the U.S. make painful cuts in its use of energy rather than permit the purchase of unused emission permits from Russia.

Meetings in Morocco in 2001 finally resulted in an emission-trading compromise that persuaded Japan to ratify the Kyoto Protocol. The compromise also seemed at first to appease Russia. In September 2003, however, Moscow decided the protocol was "scientifically flawed," and that Russia would likely not ratify it.

For a short while, there was talk among the Europeans that they might simply pursue Kyoto unilaterally—even without the United States and Russia.[2] They are still stewing over it, with some public disagreement between the EU commissioners for energy and for the environment.

There were similar calls in Washington to institute a Kyoto-like regime unilaterally. In the U.S. Senate, John McCain (R-Arizona) and Joe Lieberman (D-Connecticut) introduced a bill to do just that: a unilateral reduction of carbon dioxide

1. Buying and selling the legal rights to emit quantities of greenhouse gases.
2. Russia rejoined the treaty in 2005.

emissions over time, albeit with the possibility of emission trading and credits for carbon dioxide "sinks," like planting trees. The "McLieberman bill" (as it came to be called) failed to pass in November 2003, with senators voting mainly along party lines. . . .

Rational Environmentalism

The first and most important step toward a more sober environmental policy has to involve the underlying science. The assumptions of the global warming models must be publicly, repeatedly, and systematically critiqued, and when they do not stand up to scrutiny, these assumptions and policies must be rejected by the United States government outright.

The second step will need to be based in economics. Economists must offer convincing demonstrations of what is already apparent from the data: that modest warming correlates with increased GNP [gross national product], higher average income, and enhanced living standards across the globe; and that carbon dioxide, rather than being a pollutant, benefits the growth of agricultural crops and forests. Economists must also demonstrate that control of carbon dioxide imposes huge economic penalties, particularly on lower-income groups. This is a matter of making the facts known.

Periodical Bibliography

The following articles have been selected to supplement the diverse views presented in this chapter.

Liz Borkowski	"The Promise of the Solar Future," *Co-op America Quarterly*, Summer 2005.
Chris Clarke	"New Nukes Is Bad Nukes," *Earth Island Journal*, Summer 2005.
P. Fairly	"Solar on the Cheap," *Technology Review*, February 2002.
J. Johnson	"New Life for Nuclear Power?" *Chemical and Engineering News*, October 2, 2000.
Sara Knight	"Make Fries, Not War: Legalizing Biodiesel," *Earth Island Journal*, Autumn 2004.
Frank Kreith and Ron West	"Hydrogen Won't Be Our Energy Savior," *Boulder (CO) Daily Camera*, June 19, 2005. www.commondreams.org.
Jay Lehr	"Solar Power—Too Good to Be True," *Environment News*, June 1, 2005.
George Monbiot	"Biofuels Would Be a Disaster," *Guardian* (Manchester, UK), November 23, 2004.
Sarah Rasmussen	"Green Power to the People," *WireTap*, September 15, 2004.
Jeremy Rifkin	"The Hydrogen Economy," *E: The Environmental Magazine*, January/February 2003.
Willie Soon and Sallie Baliunas	"Wind Farms May Threaten Crop Production," Techcentralstation.com, February 1, 2005. www.tcsdaily.com.
Thomas Tanton	"A Whirlwind of Troubles—Environmental, Operational, and Financial Problems," *PERC Reports*, December 1, 2004.

How Can Natural Resources Be Conserved?

Chapter Preface

The Corporate Average Fuel Economy (CAFE) standards are fuel efficiency requirements for cars and trucks set by the U.S. government. These standards were made into law as part of the Energy Policy Conservation Act of 1975. They require that automobile makers maintain a fleet-wide fuel efficiency average set by the government. In 1978, when the standards went into effect, the requirement was 18 miles per gallon (mpg), with the goal of increasing efficiency to 27.5 mpg by 1985. As of 2006 CAFE standards are still at 27.5 mpg. Proposals to increase the standard have been repeatedly defeated in Congress. Those who argue that CAFE standards should be raised contend that higher fuel efficiency would reduce America's use of gasoline, thereby making the nation less reliant on imported oil. Critics of this stance argue that increasing the standards is not necessary because automobiles are more efficient today than at any time in their history. The controversy over CAFE standards is just one of many in the debate on how to conserve resources.

Automobiles have an enormous impact on the amount of natural resources that are used as well as the amount of emissions that are released into the atmosphere. According to the U.S. Department of Energy, transportation in the early 2000s uses about 68 percent of the 20 million barrels of oil Americans consume each day, and it accounts for about one-third of carbon emissions. Because of this, environmentalists argue that increasing CAFE standards is an effective way of conserving resources and protecting the environment. The Sierra Club, an environmental group, contends that raising CAFE standards "is the biggest single step we can take to curb global warming." Environmentalists also point out that by increasing the efficiency of automobiles, less oil will be used, which will reduce the need to drill oil in pristine places like the Arctic

National Wildlife Refuge. The Center for Auto Safety estimates that increasing CAFE standards to 45 mpg for cars and 35 mpg for light trucks would save 3 million barrels of oil each day and reduce greenhouse gas emissions by 140 million tons each year. Reducing air pollution would also positively affect public health. The Earth Policy Institute estimates that air pollution claims the lives of seventy thousand Americans each year.

Many experts, however, oppose increasing CAFE standards. The Heritage Foundation, a conservative think tank, argues that the standards have been ineffective: "Oil imports and vehicle miles driven have increased while the standards have led to reduced consumer choice and lives lost that could have survived car crashes in heavier vehicles." Writer Kimberley A. Strassel argues that "since 1970, the United States has made cars almost 50% more efficient; in that period of time, the average number of miles a person drives has doubled." The National Academy of Sciences estimates that CAFE standards cause up to 2,600 traffic deaths annually because the lighter weight of more efficient cars makes them less safe in crashes.

The debate about automobile efficiency standards shows how difficult it can be to arrive at some agreement about the best way to conserve resources.

"At only 30 years old, the Endangered Species Act has already scored major victories in species recovery."

The Endangered Species Act Is Effective

Roger Di Silvestro

Roger Di Silvestro is a senior editor for National Wildlife *magazine. In the following viewpoint Di Silvestro makes the case that the Endangered Species Act has successfully preserved endangered animal and plant species in the United States. Di Silvestro states that the success of the current law is proven by the many species that have been helped. Moreover, he believes that because the act protects the habitats of endangered species, it is good for the environment as a whole.*

As you read, consider the following questions:

1. According to this viewpoint, how many plant and animal species does the Endangered Species Act protect?
2. How many species are listed in the viewpoint as having improved due to the Endangered Species Act?
3. When, according to the author, did the first Endangered Species Act become law?

Roger Di Silvestro, "Where Would They Be Now?", *National Wildlife*, vol. 42, August-September 2004. Copyright 2004 National Wildlife Federation. Reproduced by permission.

The Endangered Species Act, which President Nixon signed into law in December 1973, was not the first of its kind. Congress had enacted two similar laws, one in 1966 and another in 1969, but neither did much more than create lists of vanishing wildlife. The 1973 law put real teeth into protecting species likely to become extinct soon. In effect, it sought to make illegal the extinction of any species from human activities.

A Pragmatic Law

That goal may sound impractical, but the law is in fact pragmatic. By seeking to protect the habitat of listed species, by funding state endangered species work and by creating a system for assessing the damage that proposed projects might do to listed species, the law spells out a practical program for protecting America's most jeopardized animals and plants.

Today the law protects more than 1,200 U.S. plant and animal species and more than 550 foreign species, some of which may provide us with such valuable assets as cures for serious illnesses and others of which simply add value to our lives through their elegance and beauty. Moreover, when we protect species, we protect habitat, and when we protect habitat—from wetlands to forests, from prairies to streams—we improve the health and safety of our own environment and that of myriad other species.

Nevertheless, the law is under assault from development interests that do not want to strike a balance with wildlife. Through their supporters in Congress and the White House, these interests seek to weaken the protections of the Endangered Species Act. They debunk the law as a failure.

As the following examples illustrate, however, the law has enjoyed demonstrable success in a relatively short time. "It took decades, in some cases centuries, to whittle away species after species until they ended up on the list," says NWF [National Wildlife Federation] endangered species specialist John

Endangered Species

Species	Observation
Plants	A quarter of the world's plants are threatened with extinction by the year 2010
Amphibians	More than 38% of US amphibians are endangered
Birds	Three-quarters of all bird species are declining; 11% are threatened with extinction
Carnivores	Almost all species of cats and bears are declining in numbers
Fish	One-third of North American freshwater fish are rare or endangered
Invertebrates	About 100 species are lost each day due to deforestation
Mammals	25% of species are threatened with extinction
Reptiles	Over 40% of reptile species are threatened, 20% with extinction

Hutchinson Encyclopedia.
Published by Helicon, 1999. www.helican.co.uk.

Kostyack. "Reversing that biological effect won't happen overnight. But at only 30 years old, the Endangered Species Act has already scored major victories in species recevery."

On the 30th anniversary of the law last year [2003], NWF and 10 other conservation groups compiled a list of 30 species that now would be much diminished or extinct if not for the law's protection. Several of these species are featured on the following pages. "In creating the Endangered Species Act in 1973, Congress recognized that plants and animals don't have to earn the right to exist, but rather that we have a responsibility to protect them," Kostyack says. "Each species is a monument to the effectiveness of the act and to those who, over the past three decades, have worked to make the law a success for wildlife and for people in their communities."

Recovered Species

Bald Eagle. As many as 100,000 bald eagles soared over the lower 48 states before Columbus reached the Americas. By 1963, hunting, habitat loss and pesticide contamination had cut the species to just 417 nesting pairs in the continental United States. Under the Endangered Species Act, the U.S. Fish and Wildlife Service (FWS) initiated captive-breeding programs and habitat protection. A 1972 DDT ban also helped. The bird now numbers nearly 6,500 pairs in the Lower 48 and may be delisted soon.

Florida Panther. Habitat loss and uncontrolled hunting reduced the Florida panther to only about 35 animals by the 1980s. Cougars once ranged in the thousands across the eastern United States, but the Florida panther is the only cougar subspecies that still survives east of the Mississippi. Protection of some vital habitat has raised the panther population to some 80 animals in recent years and also has helped other listed species, such as wood storks and eastern indigo snakes. But habitat loss persists as a critical threat.

Key Deer. A small subspecies of the white-tailed deer, the Florida Key deer once ranged throughout the keys. Uncontrolled hunting reduced the animal to only 25 individuals by 1950. One of the first species listed under the 1973 law, the deer now numbers about 500 due to habitat protection and restoration. The little animals are still jeopardized by highway construction and road kills.

Mauna Kea Silversword. High up Hawaii's Mauna Kea volcano grows the silversword, with foot-long leaves that form a rosette 2 feet in diameter. Grazing by introduced sheep and goats reduced the silversword to only 48 plants, all rooted on steep cliffs that represented only 1 percent of the species' former range. Removal of introduced animals helped raise silversword numbers to about 500.

Piping Plover. If not for the Endangered Species Act, the beleaguered piping plover might be extinct. Human activities along Atlantic and Great Lakes shores and the banks of midwestern rivers and lakes have reduced the species to only 3,000 pairs total. The law provided habitat protections that have helped to stabilize the bird, offering promise for a species in decline since the 1940s.

Florida Manatee. Crushing and drowning in canal locks, tangling in crab-trap lines and colliding with boats were among the factors that cut down the Florida manatee to about 1,000 animals by the 1960s. Measures to reduce these dangers since the species was listed in 1967 have helped bring numbers up to perhaps 3,000. But two Atlantic Coast populations that account for 80 percent of Florida's manatees still suffer a rate of mortality that makes recovery unlikely without continued protection.

Desert Tortoise. Critical habitat designations under the Endangered Species Act have protected areas vital to the desert tortoise. Although the tortoises can live as long as 100 years, they are not equipped to survive livestock grazing, off-road vehicles, mining and vandalism. FWS, the Bureau of Land Management and the National Park Service all protect land for this species.

Karner Blue Butterfly. The key to survival for the Karner blue butterfly is a flower, the wild blue lupine, that grows in pine barrens in the upper Midwest and Northeast. Development has reduced lupine numbers, robbing the Karner blue of a vital food and driving it to extinction in three states. Habitat restoration and reintroductions promise to recover the butterfly in some regions.

Gray Bat. Some 2.25 million gray bats once lived in limestone caverns in the southern and midwestern states. Human activity near the caves cut bat numbers to about 128,000 by the time the species was listed in 1976. Since then, with more caves and forests protected under the Endangered Species Act, the bat population has rebounded to an estimated 1.5 million animals.

This Law Works

These 30 species, selected by a coalition of 11 conservation groups in celebration of the 30th anniversary of the Endangered Species Act, represent the hundreds of creatures the law has snatched from the threat of extinction:

- Aleutian Canada goose
- American alligator
- Bald eagle
- Black-footed ferret
- California condor
- Chinook salmon
- Desert tortoise
- Devils Hole pupfish
- Florida manatee
- Florida panther
- Freshwater mussels
- Gray bat
- Gray wolf of the Great Lakes
- Green sea turtle
- Grizzly bear
- Karner blue butterfly

- Key deer
- Lynx in the Southern Rockies
- Masked bobwhite quail
- Mauna Kea silversword
- Peregrine falcon
- Pima pineapple cactus
- Pine Hill cactus
- Piping plover
- Red-cockaded woodpecker
- Robbins' cinquefoil
- Seabeach amaranth
- Shortnose sturgeon
- Utah prairie dog
- Whooping crane

Evolution of the Endangered Species Act

The Endangered Species Act enjoyed its first incarnation in 1966, but that law was only a weak foreshadow of the current act. Called the Endangered Species Preservation Act, it listed rare and disappearing species but gave them no protection. This law was a lot like publishing a list of murder victims but doing nothing to stop homicide.

The first effort to stem the loss of vanishing creatures came with the enactment of the 1969 Endangered Species Conservation Act, which banned the import of species threatened with worldwide extinction. But real protection did not come until the 1973 law, which is the one we live with today. It prohibits the killing or capturing of listed species or the harming of them in any way, such as through destruction of their habitat. It also forbids federal participation in projects that jeopardize listed species and calls for the protection of habitat critical to listed species.

Under this law, "endangered" designates a species in danger of extinction throughout all or a significant part of its range. "Threatened" refers to species likely to become endangered in the foreseeable future. The U.S. Fish and Wildlife Service manages the listing of land and freshwater species. The National Marine Fisheries Service is in charge of ocean species. One exception: Sea turtles are managed by the fisheries service when in the ocean but by the wildlife service when on land.

> *"The current [Endangered Species Act] pits landowners, fearful of losing use of their property, against the very species ESA is designed to protect."*

The Endangered Species Act Should Be Reformed

Nancy Marano and Ben Lieberman

Nancy Marano is a research assistant and Ben Lieberman is a senior policy analyst at the Heritage Foundation, a conservative public policy institute. The Endangered Species Act has not been effective, argue the authors in this viewpoint, because it has only helped to recover a small percentage of species listed as endangered. Furthermore, the authors claim that the act, because of the use restrictions it places on private property where endangered species are found, may encourage land owners to harm species in order to keep control of their land. Marano and Lieberman outline proposed changes to the law that they believe would reduce conflicts between the government and landowners.

As you read, consider the following questions:

1. How many plant and animal species has the Endangered Species Act rescued, according to the authors?

Nancy Marano and Ben Lieberman, "Improving the Endangered Species Act: Balancing the Needs of Landowners and Endangered Wildlife," Heritage Foundation, September 23, 2005.

2. What is the name of the new law that the authors recommend?
3. As detailed in this viewpoint, what percentage of endangered species live on private land?

The Endangered Species Act was intended to bring endangered species back from the brink, but in over 30 years it has helped rescue only 10 of the nearly 1,300 species that have been listed—a success rate of less than one percent. At the same time, the Act has dragged landowners into endless conflicts and litigation. Its vague classifications allow private property to be declared "critical habitats" almost arbitrarily, resulting in many use restrictions and seizures. The Threatened and Endangered Species Recovery Act of 2005 (H.R. 3824),[1] introduced by Rep. Richard W. Pombo (R-CA), Chairman of the House Committee on Resources, would strengthen incentives for landowners to participate in conservation, to the benefit of endangered species, while clearing up the vague classifications that put private property at risk.

Better Listings

According to U.S. Fish & Wildlife Service (FWS), 39 percent of all species listed under the Endangered Species Act (ESA) have an "unknown" status, 21 percent are "declining," and only 6 percent are "improving." This is unimpressive, and it may even be overstating ESA's success. Many species that later studies have shown should not have been listed under ESA in the first place have subsequently been moved to "stable" status, falsely suggesting improvement. Data errors account for most of these changes in classification. Historically, such errors have been responsible for the delisting of more species than evidence of reduced survival threats or actual recoveries.

After 30 years, there is still a blurred line between "threatened" and "endangered" species. About 38 percent of the spe-

1. This legislation was in committee in the U.S. Senate as of December 2005, after being passed in the U.S. House of Representatives in September 2005.

Antagonized Landowners

Nearly 80 percent of all listed species occur partially or entirely on private lands. Many analysts agree with [environmental defense attorney Michael] Bean that one overall effect of enforcing the ESA [Endangered Species Act] has been to create "unintended negative consequences, including antagonizing many of the landowners whose actions will ultimately determine the fate of many species." Bean underscored those problems in a 1994 speech at a training and education seminar sponsored by the FWS [Fish and Wildlife Service] for government employees. There is, he said, "increasing evidence that at least some private landowners are actively managing their land so as to avoid potential endangered species problems." By that, he meant the landowners are removing habitat that might attract an endangered species.

Daniel R. Simmons and Randy T. Simmons,
Regulation, *Winter 2003–2004.*

cies classified as facing a "low" threat are listed as endangered rather than threatened. This is a problem because faulty listings divert limited conservation resources from the species that need them most. Under ESA, species classification is based on the "best available" scientific data, a very vague standard that is responsible for much improper listing. Additionally, the current listing process is far from transparent, making it difficult for some stakeholders to participate. The end result is wasted resources and endless litigation.

The Threatened and Endangered Species Recovery Act of 2005 (TESRA) would clearly define the phrase "best available" data, creating more rigorous standards for scientific review, such as peer review. This would reduce the number of species listed on the basis of erroneous data and allow conservation funds to be spent more efficiently, on species that are actually endangered. As well, more precise standards would reduce the secondary economic impacts that arise due to erroneous listings.

Fewer Lawsuits

ESA has embroiled the government, as well as many landowners and conservation groups, in long-running and expensive litigation. In its most recent budget document, FWS explains that its ESA listing-related litigation workload includes 34 active lawsuits concerning some 48 species, 40 court orders concerning 88 species, and 36 notices of intent to sue concerning 104 species.

The current ESA pits landowners, fearful of losing use of their property, against the very species ESA is designed to protect. Because discovery of a snail, migratory bird, or other protected species on one's property can lead to a government taking of that property (or much of its use value), ESA gives landowners a perverse incentive to destroy evidence and habitats, rather than participate in conservation. The threat of severe restrictions on land use prompts landowners to make their lands inhospitable to rare species. However, nearly 80 percent of all species listed as endangered or threatened have habitats on private lands; engaging private landowners is not optional but critical to ensuring the survival of these species.

To that end, TESRA emphasizes private landowners' participation in species recovery and would reduce the regulatory barriers that now block state and local approaches to conservation. To begin with, TESRA changes the incentives that landowners face. By implementing species recovery agreements and providing conservation aid that rewards environmental stewardship, TESRA would benefit both landowners and species.

In addition, TESRA would bring some transparency and certainty to the takings process. Property owners would have the right to request timely written notification, due within 180 days, of whether or not any particular land use violates ESA. This is consistent with the public's "right to know." TESRA also would require that private landowners be compensated for the fair market value of any lost uses of their properties. No longer would the government be able to "take" the bulk of a property's value without compensating its owner.

TESRA would also replace the critical habitat program with a more integrated process that allows for species-specific approaches to establishing "take" prohibitions for threatened species. Without critical habitat designations, more resources could be directed to recovery plans for endangered species. This is a step in the right direction for both wildlife and property owners.

One key area of concern not addressed in TESRA is ESA's current definition of "harm." To better honor the 5th Amendment's takings clause and protect landowners, Congress should consider changing ESA's definition of harm to mean a landowner's intentional act that causes the death or physical injury of a threatened species. At present, this is poorly defined. In cases where property owners are prohibited from making modifications to their own land, or even deprived of their land entirely, it is critical that the standard be less ambiguous.

In sum, TESRA will bolster species recovery efforts by providing incentives for landowners to actively participate in conservation, eliminating flawed critical habitat designations, strengthening scientific standards, and returning decisions to the state and local governments that are better suited to address them. As well, TESRA would serve landowners by increasing openness and accountability across ESA processes and improving the protection of private property rights.

"Oil produced from the Arctic Refuge would come at enormous, and irreversible, cost."

The Arctic National Wildlife Refuge Should Be Conserved

Natural Resources Defense Council

The Natural Resources Defense Council (NRDC) is an environmental organization dedicated to preserving wildlands and wildlife. In the following viewpoint the NRDC contends that the Arctic National Wildlife Refuge is a national treasure and should not be opened for oil exploration. The Arctic Refuge is the last great American wilderness area, claims the NRDC, and should be protected. The NRDC also argues that the oil reserves in the refuge are not large enough to justify drilling, and that oil exploration would damage the refuge, contrary to what the oil industry claims.

As you read, consider the following questions:

1. According to this viewpoint, what percentage of polled Americans are said to oppose drilling in the Arctic Refuge?

Natural Resources Defense Council, "Arctic National Wildlife Refuge: A Wilderness Worth Far More than Oil," www.nrdc.org, 2005. Reproduced with permission from the Natural Resources Defense Council.

2. What percentage of daily American oil consumption do the authors claim that oil from the Arctic Refuge would supply?
3. What alternatives to oil drilling in the Arctic does this viewpoint recommend?

On the northern edge of our continent, stretching from the peaks of the Brooks Range across a vast expanse of tundra to the Beaufort Sea, lies Alaska's Arctic National Wildlife Refuge. An American Serengeti, the Arctic Refuge continues to pulse with million-year-old ecological rhythms. It is the greatest living reminder that conserving nature in its wild state is a core American value.

Now, with Congress debating the future of the Arctic Refuge, environmental advocates have scored a crucial victory. In November 2005, leaders of the House removed provisions that would have allowed drilling in the refuge from a massive budget bill.

The final bill, however, still has to be reconciled with the Senate version,[1] which would allow opening the refuge and its critical wildlife breeding grounds to oil drilling. Environmental groups and citizens across America are keeping up the pressure on Congress to demand that our representatives oppose any version of the bill that would open the Arctic Refuge to oil drilling. . . .

Americans Have Opposed Drilling in the Arctic National Wildlife Refuge

The controversy over drilling in the Arctic Refuge—the last piece of America's Arctic coastline not already open to oil exploration—isn't new. Big Oil has long sought access to the refuge's coastal plain, a fragile swath of tundra that teems with staggering numbers of birds and animals. During the Bush

1. Provisions to allow oil drilling in the Arctic National Wildlife Refuge were blocked from a bill in the U.S. Senate on December 6, 2005.

administration's first term, repeated attempts were made to open the refuge. But time after time, the American public rejected the idea. Congress has received hundreds of thousands of emails, faxes and phone calls from citizens opposed to drilling in the Arctic Refuge, an outpouring that has helped make the difference. And polls have consistently shown that a solid majority of Americans oppose drilling; a December 2004 Zogby Survey found that 55 percent of respondents oppose drilling, and that 59 percent consider attaching this issue to the budget process to be a "backdoor maneuver."

Despite repeated failure and stiff opposition, drilling proponents press on. Why? Remarks from [former] House majority leader Tom DeLay, in a closed-door session of House GOP leadership, reveal the true agenda. "It's about precedent," said DeLay. He believes that opening the Arctic Refuge will turn the corner in the broader national debate over whether or not energy, timber, mining and other industries should be allowed into pristine wild areas across the country. Next up: Greater Yellowstone? Our western canyonlands? Our coastal waters?

The drive to drill the Arctic Refuge is about oil company profits and lifting barriers to future exploration in protected lands, pure and simple. It has nothing to do with energy independence. Opening the Arctic Refuge to energy development is about transferring our public estate into corporate hands, so it can be liquidated for a quick buck.

The Arctic Refuge Oil Is a Distraction, Not a Solution

What would America gain by allowing heavy industry into the refuge? Very little. Oil from the refuge would hardly make a dent in our dependence on foreign imports—leaving our economy and way of life just as exposed to wild swings in worldwide oil prices and supply as it is today. The truth is, we simply can't drill our way to energy independence.

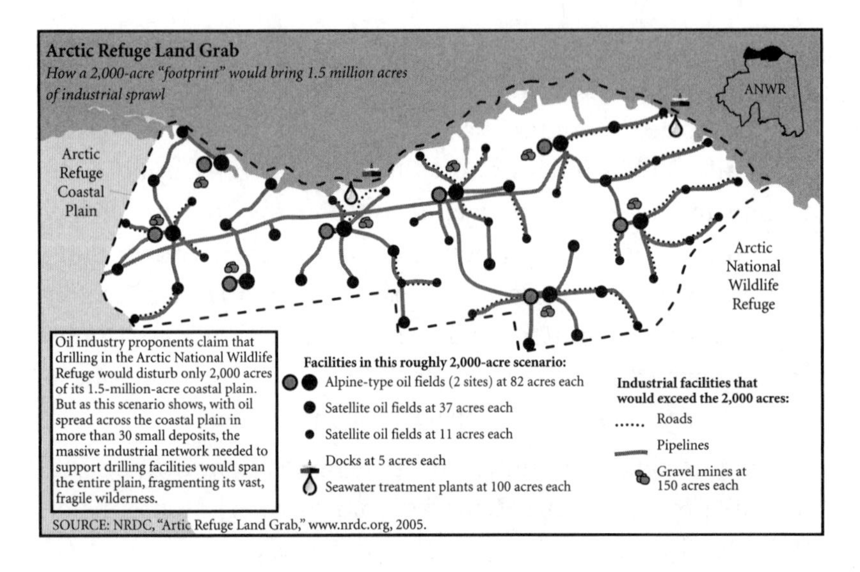

Although drilling proponents often say there are 16 billion barrels of oil under the refuge's coastal plain, the U.S. Geological Service's estimate of the amount that could be recovered economically—that is, the amount likely to be profitably extracted and sold—represents less than a year's U.S. supply.

It would take 10 years for any Arctic Refuge oil to reach the market, and even when production peaks—in the distant year of 2027—the refuge would produce a paltry 1 or 2 percent of Americans' daily consumption. Whatever oil the refuge might produce is simply irrelevant to the larger issue of meeting America's future energy needs.

Handing On to Future Generations a Wild, Pristine Arctic? Priceless.

Oil produced from the Arctic Refuge would come at enormous, and irreversible, cost. The refuge is among the world's last true wildernesses, and it is one of the largest sanctuaries for Arctic animals. Traversed by a dozen rivers and framed by jagged peaks, this spectacular wilderness is a vital birthing ground for polar bears, grizzlies, Arctic wolves, caribou and the endangered shaggy musk ox, a mammoth-like survivor of the last ice age.

For a sense of what Big Oil's heavy machinery would do to the refuge, just look 60 miles west to Prudhoe Bay—a gargantuan oil complex that has turned 1,000 square miles of fragile tundra into a sprawling industrial zone containing 1,500 miles of roads and pipelines, 1,400 producing wells and three jetports. The result is a landscape defaced by mountains of sewage, sludge, scrap metal, garbage and more than 60 contaminated waste sites that contain—and often leak—acids, lead, pesticides, solvents and diesel fuel.

While proponents of drilling insist the Arctic Refuge could be developed by disturbing as little as 2,000 acres within the 1.5-million-acre coastal plain, a recent analysis by NRDC [National Resources Defence Council] reveals this to be pure myth. Why? Because U.S. Geological Survey studies have found that oil in the refuge isn't concentrated in a single, large reservoir. Rather, it's spread across the coastal plain in more than 30 small deposits, which would require vast networks of roads and pipelines that would fragment the habitat, disturbing and displacing wildlife.

A Responsible Path to Energy Security

The solution to America's energy problems will be found in American ingenuity, not more oil. Only by reducing our reliance on oil—foreign and domestic—and investing in cleaner, renewable forms of power will our country achieve true energy security. The good news is that we already have many of the tools we need to accomplish this. For example, Detroit has the technology right now to produce high-performance hybrid cars, trucks and SUVs; if America made the transition to these more efficient vehicles, far more oil would be saved than the Arctic Refuge is likely to produce. Doesn't that make far more sense than selling out our natural heritage and exploiting one of our true wilderness gems?

VIEWPOINT

> *"Government geologists say [the Arctic National Wildlife Refuge] could hold up to 16 billion barrels of recoverable oil."*

The Arctic National Wildlife Refuge Should Be Opened for Drilling

Paul Driessen

Paul Driessen is senior policy adviser at the Center for the Defense of Free Enterprise and the author of Eco-Imperialism: Green Power, Black Death. *In the following viewpoint Driessen makes the case that the Arctic National Wildlife Refuge should be opened for oil exploration. Driessen claims that America's need for the oil reserves outweigh any negative impacts that oil drilling may have on the refuge. Oil drilling would not significantly disturb the wildlife in the area, Driessen contends, and he claims that the Native Americans in the region support drilling.*

As you read, consider the following questions:

1. How many acres in the refuge does the author claim would be required to support oil drilling?

Paul Driessen, "Support ANWR Drilling—Save Wildlife Habitats," www.ecoimperialism.com, March 28, 2005. Reproduced by permission.

2. How large is the caribou herd in the Arctic Refuge, according to this viewpoint?
3. As reported in this viewpoint, which Native Americans live in or near the refuge?

The U.S. Senate budget bill [of 2005] would finally open the Arctic National Wildlife Refuge (ANWR) to drilling. Environmentalists are shocked and outraged. "This battle is far from over," they vowed.[1]

Indeed, the 51-49 margin [in the Senate] underscores the ideological passion of drilling opponents, their party-line determination to block Bush Administration initiatives, the misinformation that still surrounds this issue, and a monumental double standard for environmental protection.

Many votes against drilling came from California and Northeastern senators who have made a career of railing against high energy prices, unemployment and balance of trade deficits—while simultaneously opposing oil and natural gas development in Alaska, the Outer Continental Shelf, western states and any other areas where petroleum might actually be found. Drilling in other countries is OK in their book, as is buying crude from oil-rich dictators, sending American jobs and dollars overseas, reducing US royalty and tax revenues, imperiling industries that depend on petroleum, and destroying habitats to generate "ecologically friendly" wind power.

This political theater of the absurd is bad enough. But many union bosses also oppose drilling, and thus kill jobs for their members—the epitome of hypocrisy.

Large Potential Reserves

Government geologists say ANWR could hold up to 16 billion barrels of recoverable oil. That's 30 years' of imports from Saudi Arabia. Turned into gasoline, it would power California's

1. As of December 2005, provisions for oil drilling in the ANWR had been blocked from legislation in the U.S. Senate.

vehicle fleet for 50 years, and hybrid and fuel cell cars would stretch the oil even further. ANWR's natural gas could fuel California's electrical generating plants for years.

At $50 a barrel, ANWR could save the US from having to import $800 billion worth of foreign oil, create up to 700,000 American jobs, and generate hundreds of billions in royalties and taxes.

No matter, say environmentalists. They claim energy development would "irreparably destroy" the refuge. Caribou doo-doo.

ANWR is the size of South Carolina: 19 million acres. Of this, only 2,000 acres along the "coastal plain" would actually be disturbed by drilling and development. That's 0.01%—one-twentieth of Washington, DC—20 of the buildings Boeing uses to manufacture its 747 jets!

The potentially oil-rich area is a flat, treeless stretch of tundra, 3,500 miles from DC and 50 miles from the beautiful mountains seen in all the misleading anti-drilling photos. During eight months of winter, when drilling would take place, virtually no wildlife are present. No wonder. Winter temperatures drop as low as minus 40 F. The tundra turns rock solid. Spit, and your saliva freezes before it hits the ground.

But the nasty conditions mean drilling can be done with ice airstrips, roads and platforms. Come spring, they'd all melt, leaving only puddles and little holes. The caribou would return—just as they have for years at the nearby Prudhoe Bay and Alpine oil fields—and do just what they always have: eat, hang out and make babies. In fact, Prudhoe's caribou herd has increased from 6,000 head in 1978 to 27,000 today. Arctic fox, geese, shore birds and other wildlife would also return, along with the Alaska state bird, *Mosquito giganteus*.

Renewable Energy Not an Alternative

But the Wilderness Society, Sierra Club, Alaska Coalition, Defenders of Wildlife, and Natural Resources Defense Council still oppose ANWR development—even as they promote their favorite alternative to Arctic oil: wind energy. Electricity from wind is hardly a substitute for petroleum—especially for cars, trains, boats and planes. And swapping reliable, revenue-generating petroleum for intermittent, tax-subsidized wind power is a poor tradeoff.

On ecological grounds, wind power fails even more miserably.

A single 555-megawatt gas-fired power plant on 15 acres generates more electricity each year than do all 13,000 of California's wind turbines—which dominate 106,000 acres of once-scenic hill country. They kill some 10,000 eagles, hawks, other birds and bats every year.

On West Virginia's Backbone Mountain, 44 turbines killed numerous birds and 2,000 bats in 2003—and promoters want many more towers along this major migratory route over the Allegheny Front. Bat Conservation International and local politicians are livid.

In Wisconsin, anti-oil groups support building 133 gigantic Cuisinarts on 32,000 acres (16 times the ANWR operations area) near Horicon Marsh. This magnificent wetland is home to millions of geese, ducks and other migratory birds, and just miles from an abandoned mine that houses 140,000 bats. At 390 feet in height, the turbines tower over the Statue of Liberty (305 feet), US capitol (287 feet) and Arctic oil production facilities (50 feet).

All these turbines would produce about as much power as Fairfax County, Virginia gets from one facility that burns garbage to generate electricity. But they'd likely crank out an amazing amount of goose liver paté.

In Maryland's mountains, off the Cape Cod coast, amidst the tall grass prairie country of Kansas and elsewhere, the tradeoff is the same: thousands of flying mammals and tens of thousands of acres sacrificed to wind power, to "save" ANWR. Better yet, America could generate nearly 20% of its electricity

Chuck Asay. © 2001 Creators Syndicate, Inc. Reproduced by permission of Chuck Asay and Creators Syndicate, Inc.

from the wind, says the American Wind Energy Association, if it devoted just 1% of its land mass to these turbines. What's 1% of the USA, you ask. It's the state of Virginia: 23,000,000 acres.

The alternative to no wind energy and no Arctic oil is equally untenable: freeze jobless in the dark, or spend countless billions to import still more oil from the likes of Hugo Chavez and the mullahs of Iran.

Native Americans Approve

The hypocrisy of this ecological double standard is palpable. So union bosses, greens and liberal politicians bring up the Gwich'in Indians, who claim drilling would "threaten their traditional lifestyle."

Inuit Eskimos who live in ANWR support drilling by an 8:1 margin. They're tired of living in poverty and using

5-gallon pails for toilets—after having given up their land claims for oil rights that Congress has repeatedly denied them.

The Gwich'ins live 150–250 miles away—and their reservations about drilling aren't exactly carved in stone. Back in the 1980s, the Alaska Gwich'ins leased 1.8 million acres of their tribal lands for oil development. That's more land than has been proposed for exploration in ANWR. (No oil was found.)

A couple years ago, Canada's Gwich'ins announced plans to drill in their 1.4-million-acre land claims area. The proposed drill sites (and a potential pipeline route) are just east of a major migratory path, where caribou often birth their calves, before they arrive in ANWR.

Many therefore suspect that the Gwich'ins role as anti-oil poster children has a lot to do with the fact that they have received at least $630,000 from the Wilderness Society and a herd of liberal foundations. In exchange, they've placed full-page ads in major newspapers, appeared in television spots and testified on Capitol Hill in opposition to ANWR exploration—while pursuing their own drilling programs.

Alternative energy technologies are certainly coming. Just ponder how we traveled, heated our homes, communicated and manufactured things 100 years ago—versus today. But the change won't happen overnight. Nor will it come via government mandates, or by throwing an anti-oil monkey wrench into our economy.

It shouldn't come at the expense of habitats, scenery and wildlife, either. Anyone who cares about these things should support automotive R&D [research and development]—and ANWR oil development.

VIEWPOINT 

"If properly developed, disseminated, and used, genetically modified crops might well be the best hope the planet has got."

Modern Agricultural Practices Conserve Resources

Jonathan Rauch

Jonathan Rauch is a writer in residence at the Brookings Institution and the author of Government's End: Why Washington Stopped Working. *Rauch contends in the following viewpoint that biotechnology may help conserve natural resources by increasing crop yields and thus reducing the amount of land that is converted to farmland. Rauch points out that agricultural practices greatly impact the environment. Genetically modified organisms, which are created to withstand herbicides and soil salinity, might enable farmers to use fewer chemicals, better prevent soil erosion and damage, and ultimately spare forest lands from cultivation, according to the author.*

As you read, consider the following questions:

1. When, as discussed in this viewpoint, does the United Nations predict world population will stop increasing?
2. How does the author define "biotech"?

Jonathan Rauch, "Will Frankenfood Save the Planet?", *The Atlantic Monthly*, October 2003, pp. 103–107.

3. How many square miles of wildlife habitat, according to Rauch, have been saved due to agricultural technology improvements since 1950?

That genetic engineering may be the most environmentally beneficial technology to have emerged in decades, or possibly centuries, is not immediately obvious. Certainly, at least, it is not obvious to the many U.S. and foreign environmental groups that regard biotechnology as a bête noire [literally "black beast," or something disliked]. Nor is it necessarily obvious to people who grew up in cities, and who have only an inkling of what happens on a modern farm. . . .

Agriculture and the Planet

It is only a modest exaggeration to say that as goes agriculture, so goes the planet. Of all the human activities that shape the environment, agriculture is the single most important, and it is well ahead of whatever comes second. Today about 38 percent of the earth's land area is cropland or pasture—a total that has crept upward over the past few decades as global population has grown. The increase has been gradual, only about 0.3 percent a year; but that still translates into an additional Greece or Nicaragua cultivated or grazed every year.

Farming does not go easy on the earth, and never has. To farm is to make war upon millions of plants (weeds, so-called) and animals (pests, so-called) that in the ordinary course of things would crowd out or eat or infest whatever it is a farmer is growing. Crop monocultures, as whole fields of only wheat or corn or any other single plant are called, make poor habitat and are vulnerable to disease and disaster. Although fertilizer runs off and pollutes water, farming without fertilizer will deplete and eventually exhaust the soil. Pesticides can harm the health of human beings and kill desirable or harmless bugs along with pests. Irrigation leaves behind trace elements that can accumulate and poison the soil. And on and on.

The trade-offs are fundamental. Organic farming, for example, uses no artificial fertilizer, but it does use a lot of manure, which can pollute water and contaminate food. Traditional farmers may use less herbicide, but they also do more ploughing, with all the ensuing environmental complications. Low-input agriculture uses fewer chemicals but more land. The point is not that farming is an environmental crime—it is not—but that there is no escaping the pressure it puts on the planet.

Feeding a Growing Population

In the next half century the pressure will intensify. The United Nations [UN], in its midrange projections, estimates that the earth's human population will grow by more than 40 percent, from 6.3 billion people today to 8.9 billion in 2050. Feeding all those people, and feeding their billion or so hungry pets (a dog or a cat is one of the first things people want once they move beyond a subsistence lifestyle), and providing the increasingly protein-rich diets that an increasingly wealthy world will expect—doing all of that will require food output to at least double, and possibly triple.

But then the story will change. According to the UN's midrange projections (which may, if anything, err somewhat on the high side), around 2050 the world's population will more or less level off. Even if the growth does not stop, it will slow. The crunch will be over. In fact, if in 2050 crop yields are still increasing, if most of the world is economically developed, and if population pressures are declining or even reversing—all of which seems reasonably likely—then the human species may at long last be able to feed itself, year in and year out, without putting any additional net stress on the environment. We might even be able to grow everything we need while *reducing* our agricultural footprint: returning cropland to wilderness, repairing damaged soils, restoring ecosystems, and so on. In other words, human agriculture might be placed on a sustainable footing forever: a breathtaking prospect.

The great problem, then, is to get through the next four or five decades with as little environmental damage as possible. That is where biotechnology comes in. . . .

Biotechnology

"Biotech" can refer to a number of things, but the relevant application here is genetic modification: the selective transfer of genes from one organism to another. Ordinary breeding can cross related varieties, but it cannot take a gene from a bacterium, for instance, and transfer it to a wheat plant. The organisms resulting from gene transfers are called "transgenic" by scientists—and "Frankenfood" by many greens.

Gene transfer poses risks, unquestionably. So, for that matter, does traditional crossbreeding. But many people worry that transgenic organisms might prove more unpredictable. One possibility is that transgenic crops would spread from fields into forests or other wild lands and there become environmental nuisances, or worse. A further risk is that transgenic plants might cross-pollinate with neighboring wild plants, producing "superweeds" or other invasive or destructive varieties in the wild. Those risks are real enough that even most biotech enthusiasts . . . favor some government regulation of transgenic crops.

What is much less widely appreciated is biotech's potential to do the environment good. Take as an example continuous no-till farming, which really works best with the help of transgenic crops. Human beings have been ploughing for so long that we tend to forget why we started doing it in the first place. The short answer: weed control. Turning over the soil between plantings smothers weeds and their seeds. If you don't plough, your land becomes a weed garden—unless you use herbicides to kill the weeds. Herbicides, however, are expensive, and can be complicated to apply. And they tend to kill the good with the bad.

In the mid-1990s the agricultural-products company Monsanto introduced a transgenic soybean variety called Roundup Ready. As the name implies, these soybeans tolerate Roundup, an herbicide (also made by Monsanto) that kills many kinds of weeds and then quickly breaks down into harmless ingredients. Equipped with Roundup Ready crops, farmers found that they could retire their ploughs and control weeds with just a few applications of a single, relatively benign herbicide—instead of many applications of a complex and expensive menu of chemicals. More than a third of all U.S. soybeans are now grown without ploughing, mostly owing to the introduction of Roundup Ready varieties. Ploughless cotton farming has likewise received a big boost from the advent of bioengineered varieties. No-till farming without biotech is possible, but it's more difficult and expensive, which is why no-till and biotech are advancing in tandem.

Transgenic Tomatoes

In 2001 a group of scientists announced that they had engineered a transgenic tomato plant able to thrive on salty water—water, in fact, almost half as salty as seawater, and fifty times as salty as tomatoes can ordinarily abide. One of the researchers was quoted as saying, "I've already transformed tomato, tobacco, and canola. I believe I can transform any crop with this gene"—just the sort of Frankenstein hubris that makes environmentalists shudder. But consider the environmental implications. Irrigation has for millennia been a cornerstone of agriculture, but it comes at a price. As irrigation water evaporates, it leaves behind traces of salt, which accumulate in the soil and gradually render it infertile. (As any Roman legion knows, to destroy a nation's agricultural base you salt the soil.) Every year the world loses about 25 million acres—an area equivalent to a fifth of California—to salinity;

The Green Revolution

From 1950 to 1992, the world's grain output rose from 692 million tons produced on 1.70 billion acres of cropland to 1.9 billion tons on 1.73 billion acres of cropland—an increase in yield of more than 150 percent. Without high-yield agriculture, either millions would have starved or increases in food output would have been realized only through drastic expansion of acres under cultivation—with losses of pristine wilderness a hundred times greater than all the losses to urban and suburban expansion.

Today, we confront a similar problem: feeding the anticipated global population of more than eight billion people in the coming quarter of a century. The world has or will soon have the agricultural technology available to meet this challenge. The new biotechnology can help us to do things that we could not do before, and to do it in a more precise, predicable, and efficient way.

Norman Borlaug,
Foreword to The Frankenfood Myth
by Henry I. Miller and Gregory Con Ko, 2004.

40 percent of the world's irrigated land, and 25 percent of America's, has been hurt to some degree. For decades traditional plant breeders tried to create salt-tolerant crop plants, and for decades they failed.

Salt-tolerant crops might bring millions of acres of wounded or crippled land back into production.

Biotech Cotton

One of the first biotech crops to reach the market, in the mid-1990s, was a cotton plant that makes its own pesticide. Scientists incorporated into the plant a toxin-producing gene from a soil bacterium known as *Bacillus thuringiensis.* With Bt cotton, as it is called, farmers can spray much less, and the poison contained in the plant is delivered only to bugs that actually eat the crop. As any environmentalist can tell you, insecticide is not very nice stuff—especially if you breathe it, which many Third World farmers do as they walk through their fields with backpack sprayers.

Transgenic cotton reduced pesticide use by more than two million pounds in the United States from 1996 to 2000, and it has reduced pesticide sprayings in parts of China by more than half. Earlier this year [2003] the Environmental Protection Agency approved a genetically modified corn that resists a beetle larva known as rootworm. Because rootworm is American corn's most voracious enemy, this new variety has the potential to reduce annual pesticide use in America by more than 14 million pounds. It could reduce or eliminate the spraying of pesticide on 23 million acres of U.S. land.

All of that is the beginning, not the end. Bioengineers are also working, for instance, on crops that tolerate aluminum, another major contaminant of soil, especially in the tropics. Return an acre of farmland to productivity, or double yields on an already productive acre, and, other things being equal, you reduce by an acre the amount of virgin forest or savannah that will be stripped and cultivated. That may be the most important benefit of all.

Farming to Save Forests

Of the many people I have interviewed in my twenty years as a journalist, Norman Borlaug must be the one who has saved the most lives. Today he is an unprepossessing eighty-nine-year-old man of middling height, with crystal-bright blue eyes and thinning white hair. He still loves to talk about plant breeding, the discipline that won him the 1970 Nobel Peace Prize: Borlaug led efforts to breed the staples of the Green Revolution. Yet the renowned plant breeder is quick to mention that he began his career, in the 1930s, in forestry, and that forest conservation has never been far from his thoughts. In the 1960s, while he was working to improve crop yields in India and Pakistan, he made a mental connection. He would create tables detailing acres under cultivation and average yields—and then, in another column, he would estimate how much land had been saved by higher farm productivity. Later, in the 1980s and 1990s, he and others began paying increased attention to what some agricultural economists now call the Borlaug hypothesis: that the Green Revolution has saved not only many human lives but, by improving the productivity of existing farmland, also millions of acres of tropical forest and other habitat—and so has saved countless animal lives.

From the 1960s through the 1980s, for example, Green Revolution advances saved more than 100 million acres of wild lands in India. More recently, higher yields in rice, coffee, vegetables, and other crops have reduced or in some cases stopped forest-clearing in Honduras, the Philippines, and elsewhere. [There are] that if farming techniques and yields had not improved since 1950, the world would have lost an additional 20 million or so square miles of wildlife habitat, most of it forest. About 16 million square miles of forest exists today. . . .

The Future Challenge

Habitat destruction remains a serious environmental problem; in some respects it is the most serious. The savannahs and tropical forests of Central and South America, Asia, and Africa by and large make poor farmland, but they are the earth's storehouses of biodiversity, and the forests are the earth's lungs. Since 1972 about 200,000 square miles of Amazon rain forest have been cleared for crops and pasture; from 1966 to 1994 all but three of the Central American countries cleared more forest than they left standing. Mexico is losing more than 4,000 square miles of forest a year to peasant farms; sub-Saharan Africa is losing more than 19,000.

That is why the great challenge of the next four or five decades is not to feed an additional three billion people (and their pets) but to do so without converting much of the world's prime habitat into second- or third-rate farmland. Now, most agronomists agree that some substantial yield improvements are still to be had from advances in conventional breeding, fertilizers, herbicides, and other Green Revolution standbys. But it seems pretty clear that biotechnology holds more promise—probably much more. Recall that world food output will need to at least double and possibly triple over the next several decades. Even if production could be increased that much using conventional technology, which is doubtful, the required amounts of pesticide and fertilizer and other polluting chemicals would be immense. If properly developed, disseminated, and used, genetically modified crops might well be the best hope the planet has got.

> *"American industrial farming uses close to one billion pounds of pesticides to produce a truly toxic harvest."*

Modern Agricultural Practices Do Not Conserve Resources

Christopher D. Cook

Christopher D. Cook is an investigative journalist and the author of Diet for a Dead Planet: How the Food Industry Is Killing Us, *from which the following viewpoint was excerpted. In it Cook argues that modern agricultural practices are damaging the environment through the prolific use of chemical pesticides, herbicides, and fertilizers. Moreover, there is little evidence, Cook claims, that biotechnology will reduce the need for agricultural chemicals in the future. Cook concludes that organic farming, which does not utilize synthetic herbicides, pesticides, and fertilizers, should be pursued.*

As you read, consider the following questions:

1. According to this viewpoint, what increase in the use of pesticides has been observed since 1991?
2. How many birds per year does Cook claim are killed by agricultural pesticides?

Christopher D. Cook, *Diet for a Dead Planet*, The New Press, New York, 2004. Chapter 9: "Killing Fields: The Spraying of America," pp. 160–173.

3. How large was the dead zone in the Gulf of Mexico in 1999, as discussed in this viewpoint?

When [biologist] Rachel Carson published *Silent Spring* in 1962, the American pesticide business was in full postwar bloom. These "elixirs of death" were suddenly ubiquitous, their use growing from 124 million pounds in 1947 to 637 million by 1960, a fivefold increase. Roughly 60 percent, about 375 million pounds, of these synthetic potions were applied to farmlands. Toxic residues from pesticides were indeed everywhere: in most of the major rivers and groundwater; "lodged in the bodies of fish, birds, reptiles, and domestic and wild animals"; "stored in the bodies of the vast majority of human beings"; found even in that most sacred nectar, mother's milk. DDT, a now-infamous poison originally thought to be harmless after it was sprayed on soldiers and prisoners to kill lice, with no immediately obvious harm, was "so universally used that in most minds the product take son the harmless aspect of the familiar. . . ."

Beginning in the mid-1950s, as towns and beautification-conscious (and mosquito-fearing) suburbs lavished more pesticides on parks and tree-lined streets, scientists recorded a mounting toll of dead birds. One analysis in Wisconsin reported a robin mortality rate of more than 86 percent in sprayed areas. Laboratories in Michigan and elsewhere were overloaded with robin carcasses; one woman called a lab to report a dozen dead robins lying in her lawn. It was, truly, a silent spring, eerily devoid of the orchestra of birdsong that had always heralded winter's thaw.

The heavy rain of pesticides on farms created silent streams, as well. The contamination of groundwater by pesticide-soaked soils and irrigation canals became a hidden threat to entire water systems. As Carson explained, "It is not possible to add pesticides to water anywhere without threatening the purity of water everywhere." In one case, "A sample of drinking water from an orchard area in Pennsylvania, when tested on fish in a laboratory, contained enough insecticide to kill all of the test fish in only four hours." In another instance, "Water from a stream draining sprayed cotton fields remained lethal to fishes even after it had passed through a purifying plant." In Alabama, runoff from sprayed fields killed all the fish in fifteen tributaries to the Tennessee River. . . .

Pesticides Today

True, some of the most vicious so-called "dirty dozen" pesticides, such as DDT and chlordane, were banished (only to resurface soon thereafter in developing countries such as Mexico). Yet, with little fanfare, American industrial farming uses close to *one billion pounds* of pesticides to produce a truly toxic harvest. The food industry, particularly the biotechnology sector, benefits from a decided hush when it comes to today's silent spring. Unless you read government reports or devour the reams of studies on the environmental and human-health effects of pesticides, you might think pesticides were just an unfortunate industrial episode of the past.

Now, in the brave new high-tech world of engineered crops that, like the Monsanto potato, emit their own pesticides from the inside out, we needn't worry ourselves with outmoded notions of poisoned farmworkers, pesticide drift, and children munching on toxic apples. The U.S. Department of Agriculture and corporate biotech officials have claimed publicly that genetically modified crops are helping to cleanse the environment by reducing pesticides. Addressing the UN Food and Agriculture Organization's thirty-first annual conference in November 2001, U.S. Secretary of Agriculture Ann Veneman said the "technologies of the new century," namely biotechnology and information technology, promise to "make agriculture more environmentally sustainable." The facts show otherwise.

Despite public assurances that agriculture is now kinder and gentler, the reality is that the biotech and chemical industries march hand in hand as two sides of one corporate coin.

The industry's most prominent genetically modified organism (GMO), Monsanto's "Roundup Ready" soybean, was designed to withstand intensive spraying, and thus expanded sales, of the firm's highly popular, and highly toxic, herbicide Roundup. Since the 1996 introduction of Roundup Ready, the use of glyphosate, a key Roundup ingredient that studies have linked to non-Hodgkin's lymphoma, has risen. "Industry claims that the use of genetic engineering in agriculture is environmentally sound and will reduce the use of agro-chemicals. But this is clearly not the case" says Sarojeni V. Rengam, executive director of the Pesticide Action Network's Asia and Pacific branch. "They will only perpetuate and possibly increase the use of herbicides, especially glyphosate, as can be seen from the U.S. example." . . .

Vicious Circle of Spraying

After a modest decline in the 1980s, the amount of pesticides used each year has increased by more than 100 million pounds since 1991. Farm pesticide use shot up by 75 million pounds in 1994 alone. Simultaneously there's been a dramatic increase in pesticide costs borne by farmers, whose spending on herbicides has more than doubled since 1980. Meanwhile the use of pesticides has declined in all other sectors. In 1964, 59 percent of all U.S. pesticides were used in agriculture; by 1997 the figure was 80 percent. Each year in California alone, over 100 million pounds of highly toxic active ingredients from pesticides are released into the environment.

Why has pesticide use increased even in this time of growing ecological awareness? In *Living Downstream*, biologist and cancer survivor Sandra Steingraber describes the political economy that has driven agriculture into a self-feeding cycle of poison. First, the arrival of synthetic pesticides following World War II reduced labor on the farm. Simultaneously, profits per acre began to shrivel. "Both these changes pressed farmers into managing more acres to earn a living for their families,"says Steingraber. Bigger farms, and federal subsidies promoting monocrop agriculture "further increased the need for chemicals to control pests. And the use of these chemicals themselves set the stage for additional ecological changes that only more chemicals could offset."

The planting of the same crop, and only one crop, year after year enables insect populations to adapt and recover, intensifying the upward chemical spiral. Steingraber describes the process: "Eradicating insects with pesticides incites more severe pest outbreaks"; through natural selection, the few insects able to repel insecticides "become the progenitors of the next generation as their more chemically sensitive compatriots are killed off"; thus pesticides ultimately encourage genetic resistance. During the postwar pesticide revolution between 1950 and 1990, the number of insect species resistant to pesticides mushroomed from fewer than 20 to more than 500. In roughly the same period, the amount of crops lost due to insect damage doubled. . . .

Effects on Birds, Fish, and Frogs

Spring, if not silent, is no doubt quieter for the continued onslaught of pesticides on birds, which threatens ecologies and trims the ranks of endangered species. Every year agricultural pesticides alone kill an estimated 67 million birds. An array of disturbing side effects is in store for those "lucky" enough to survive a sublethal dose, including weight loss, "increased susceptibility to predation, decreased disease resistance, lack of interest in mating and defending territory, and abandonment of nestlings," stated a 1999 report by Californians for Pesticide Reform and the Pesticide Action Network.

A key indicator of today's pesticide pollution epidemic lies underground, in the hidden waters that ultimately percolate up into rivers, lakes, and wells. Groundwater, the source of 50 percent of America's drinking water, is intimately interconnected with surface water: "As water seeps through the soil, it carries with it substances applied to the land, such as fertilizers and pesticides." As Carson wrote in 1962, "Pollution of the groundwater is pollution of water everywhere." . . .

Nationwide reports are equally troubling, revealing a bath of chemicals that, though often at low levels individually, combine in a toxic soup harmful to fish and the broader freshwater ecosystem. In a ten-year study in which it examined thousands of streams across the country, the United States GeologicalSurvey traced the proliferation of numerous agricultural pesticides: atrazine was present in 90 percent of the streams; two others, deethylatrazine and metolachlor, were in 82 percent of all samples; others were detected in at least 40 percent of the samples. Still more disquieting was a 1999 USGS finding that there was an average of twenty pesticides, mostly agricultural, at each river or stream tested. Chemical concentrations of some compounds "frequently were higher than the quality standards and criteria established for these compounds in drinking water," and one or more standards for protecting aquatic life were exceeded in thirty-nine of fifty-eight sites.

The overall picture is clear: Over the past thirty years, nearly half of all pesticides targeted for research by numerous studies have been found in stream sediment and in some 64 percent of edible fish, mollusks, and other freshwater aquatic life.

Even when fish are not directly poisoned, they commonly ingest toxins from the plants they eat, which are often marinated in pesticide residues. Scientists are increasingly observing important changes in the hormones and reproductive systems in fish and other aquatic creatures exposed to pesticides. One study of sex hormones in carp revealed that the ratio of estrogen to testosterone, in both males and females, was "significantly lower at sites with the highest pesticide concentrations." Pesticides may also be a factor behind rising numbers of frog deformities, such as extra or missing limbs. In a 2002 study published in the *Proceedings of the National Academy of Sciences*, the biologist Joseph Kiesecker compared frogs in Pennsylvania ponds that had pesticide runoff with those in ponds that did not. The rate of misshapen frogs was nearly four times higher in the ponds with pesticides. . . .

A Dead Zone in the Gulf

Hypoxia sounds like a teenage skin problem. It is really the cause of a "dead zone" in the Gulf of Mexico, stretching across several thousand square miles along the Louisiana-Texas coast. Here, a massive algae bloom feasts on a steady diet of nitrogen and other nutrients that flow down the Mississippi River and into the Gulf. In summer, when the river's flow peaks, the algae spread like an oil spill and choke the Gulf's northern coasts, cutting off oxygen that supports sea life. In 1999 the zone expanded to nearly 12,500 square miles, an area greater than the size of New Jersey. The oxygen-depleted water near the floor of the Gulf here contains less than two parts per million of dissolved oxygen, not enough to sustain fish and bottom-dwelling life.

One of the chief culprits behind this dead zone is American agriculture and its countless tributaries of fertilizer, pesticides, and animal feces. The Mississippi River Basin, which drains an area representing about 41 percent of the contiguous United States, is home to the majority of the nation's agricultural chemicals. About 7 million metric tons of nitrogen in commercial fertilizers are applied in the Mississippi Basin each year. These substances are the precursors of nitrates, which function as nutrients for algae blooms. Algae use up available oxygen and prevent the water from becoming reoxygenated. Since the late 1950s, when pesticides and synthetic fertilizers began to dominate the agricultural scene, the annual load of nitrates poured from the Mississippi River into the Gulf has tripled. According to the USGS, "The largest change in annual nitrogen input has been in fertilizer, which has in-

Zero-Pesticide Farming

Modern farmers have come to depend on a great variety of insecticides, herbicides, and fungicides to control the pests, weeds, and diseases that threaten crop and animal productivity. Though integrated pest management dates back to the 1950s, a significant paradigm-shifting moment occurred in the early 1980s when Peter Kenmore and his colleagues in Southeast Asia found—contrary to what might be expected—that pest attack on rice was directly proportional to the amount of pesticides used.

The reason for the pest population increase was simple: Pesticides were killing the natural enemies of insect pests, such as spiders and beetles,and were also causing the spread of resistance among the pests. When pest predators are eliminated from agroecosystems, pests are able to expand innumbers very rapidly.

Jules Pretty, Environment, *November 2003.*

creased more than six fold since the 1950s." Another key nitrate source that is on the rise is the millions of tons of factory-farm animal waste. . . .

The Petrochemical Addiction

It doesn't have to be this way. Agriculture can be prolific and-efficient without pesticides. In fact, the miraculous march of American agriculture toward unparalleled productivity long before the postwar pesticide revolution is a compelling testimonial to the effectiveness of organic farming. Before agribusiness and its petrochemical addiction, farmers used crop rotation and diversified agriculture to replenish soils and keep pests on the run. Crop diversity supplied sustenance for farm families and livestock, and was a natural insurance policy against pest outbreaks or weather disasters. "Growing many different types of crops over the years in the same field," writes Miguel A. Altieri, an agroecology expert, "also suppressed insects, weeds, and diseases by effectively breaking the life cycles of these pests."

Although many conventional growers have bravely jumped the toxic ship and transitioned into organics—a lengthy, costly process for which there is virtually no government support—the current food economy and agribusiness profits rely on farmers' continued deployment of chemical warfare in the fields. The near-perennial American surplus fueled by petrochemicals keeps farm crops cheap, not so much for consumers as for the intermediary complex of food processors, fast-food chains, and supermarkets.

It's important to note that surplus preceded pesticides. Back in the *Silent Spring* days, the United States was already stockpiling surplus, with concomitant increasing subsidy payments to farmers and growing pressures on exports and food aid. As Rachel Carson remarked then, "We are told that the enormous and expanding use of pesticides is necessary to maintain farm production." Yet, noting that American taxpayers then were paying more than $1 billion a year for surplus food storage alone, she asked pointedly, "Is our real problem not one of over-production?" Excess supply is indeed a problem for farmers, who, disciplined by the market, must "get big or get out." For the petrochemical industry and its close partner, the biotech business, however, today's system of overproduction, and of toxic industrial agriculture stripped of its natural sustainability, is not a problem at all but a precondition for profit. Except that they (and their children) must also inhabit a poisoned world.

Periodical Bibliography

The following articles have been selected to supplement the diverse views presented in this chapter.

Charli E. Coon	"Why the Government's CAFE Standards for Fuel Efficiency Should Be Repealed, Not Increased," July 11, 2001. www.heritage.org.
Myron Ebell	"An Update on Endangered Species Act Reform," *ALEC Policy Forum*, May 5, 2005. www.cei.org.
Michael T. Klare	"Arctic Drilling Is No Energy Answer," *Los Angeles Times*, April 3, 2005.
Amory B. Lovins	"More Profit with Less Carbon," *Scientific American*, September 2005.
Henry I. Miller	"Biotech Food Is Safe, Widely Used," *Environment News*, June 1, 2004.
Ralph Nader	"Spinning Wheels—Our Continual Refusal to Raise CAFE Standards," April 12, 2004. www.commondreams.org.
Julia Olmstead	"Our Reckless Chemical Dependence," August 23, 2005. www.commondreams.org.
Reason Foundation	"Arctic National Wildlife Refuge," April 2005. www.reason.org.
Perry Schmeiser	"Theft of Life," *Resurgence*, March/April 2004.
Vandana Shiva	"Biotech Wars: Food Freedom Versus Food Slavery," *E: The Environmental Magazine*, July 23, 2003.
Kimberley A. Strassel	"Conservation Wastes Energy," *Wall Street Journal*, May 17, 2001.

CHAPTER

What Can Institutions and Individuals Do to Conserve?

Chapter Preface

Americans own nearly 2 billion consumer electronics items, including televisions, personal computers, cell phones, and stereos. The advance of computer technology brings constant improvements to many of these products, which makes the current models obsolete as new models enter the marketplace. Many analysts contend that this high-tech waste damages the environment. As writer Elizabeth Grossman notes, "This digital wizardry relies on a complex array of materials—metals, elements, plastics, and chemical compounds. Each tidy piece of equipment has a story that begins in mines, refineries, factories, rivers, and aquifers, and ends on pallets and in dumpsters, smelters, and landfills all around the world." How to deal with high-tech waste is one of many debates about how society can protect the environment.

High-tech waste, or e-waste as it is sometimes called, presents disposal challenges. The sheer quantity of material being discarded indicates the scope of the problem. The Environmental Protection Agency (EPA) estimates that Americans throw away over 2 million tons of high-tech electronics each year. The EPA also estimates that between 2003 and 2010 Americans will discard 200 million televisions and 250 million computers. This is on top of the sixty-five thousand tons of cell phones that were predicted to be discarded by 2005. Because much of the waste is toxic, disposing of it safely is more difficult than getting rid of other trash. For instance, a cathode-ray tube computer monitor contains between five and eight pounds of lead. As writer Harvey Blatt points out, "The estimated 315 million computers that were obsolete by 2004 contain an estimated 1.2 billion pounds of lead." Lead can cause nerve problems if ingested by people. Electronic equipment also contains other materials that can become toxic substances when thrown into landfills. Electronics are considered by the EPA to be hazardous waste.

One idea for addressing e-waste is called extended producer responsibility (EPR). With EPR, producers of electronic equipment are required by law to take responsibility for how the equipment will be disposed of or recycled. This disposal activity has traditionally been the responsibility of consumers and local governments. The Organization for Economic Cooperation and Development (OECD) states that a goal of EPR is "to provide incentives to producers to take environmental considerations into the design of the product." In 2004 the European Union (EU) passed EPR regulations requiring manufacturers of electronic products to take back and recycle their products, financed by a fee built into the price of new items.

Not everyone agrees that EPR would be effective. Jacques Fonteyne of the European Recovery and Recycling Organization (ERRA) contends that if "individual manufacturers become responsible for collection, sorting, and recovery or disposal of their own products, there will be a tendency toward a separate, parallel, or segregated waste management system." This disposal system, he argues, would be "less efficient, both economically and environmentally." Lynn Scarlett of the Reason Foundation claims that the "critical part of the recycling equation is cost. Transport and disassembly costs can be high—as much as $10–$15 just to ship a computer." EPR regulations could thus cause higher costs for consumer products.

Whether EPR will become the norm worldwide is debatable. The authors in the following chapter discuss other ways in which individuals and institutions can help conserve the environment.

Viewpoint 1

> *"If efforts at population control fail and we continue to grow dramatically as a species, we will find ourselves facing various shortages."*

Curbing Human Population Growth Will Help Conserve the Environment

Ed McGaa

Ed McGaa, a lawyer, was born on the Oglala Sioux reservation in South Dakota. He is the author of several books including Nature's Way: Native Wisdom for Living in Balance with the Earth, *from which the following viewpoint was excerpted. McGaa argues in this viewpoint that human overpopulation is the root cause of many environmental problems. McGaa proposes that governments address overpopulation by attending to women's issues. In many poor nations, women do not have access to birth control, for example, and their lower status results in their inability to control the size of their families, McGaa contends.*

Ed McGaa, *Nature's Way: Native Wisdom for Living in Balance with the Earth*, HarperCollins, 2004.

As you read, consider the following questions:

1. According to this viewpoint, by how many people has population in the United States increased since 1970?
2. How many women die each year due to unwanted pregnancy complications, as discussed by the author?
3. How much land, according to McGaa, is required to support each person living in a first world city?

While Earth is facing the sixth great extinction of its plants and animals, Earth's human population is competing with non-human species for survival. Amazingly like rats in our choice of populated habitat, 20 percent of the world's people live on the 12 percent of the land surface with the highest densities of non-human species. Human population is growing at an annual rate of 1.8 percent in these biodiversity hotspots—significantly faster than the 1.3 percent rate in the world as a whole—and is threatening habitats and endangering species.

The Iroquois people consider such human overpopulation to be irresponsible toward our plant and our animal relations. Throughout many generations since the late 1500s the population of the Iroquois in New York has remained constant at about 200,000 people. They have a saying: "The frog does not drink up the pond in which it lives."

As Linda DeStefano notes in an article for the *Syracuse Herald-American*, it took all of recorded history until 1830 for world population to reach one billion; by 1930 we were at two billion; by 1960, three billion; 1975, four billion; 1986, five billion; and in 1999 we crossed the six billion mark. The world is adding about 78 million more people every year. The United Nations Population Fund has projected that the world population will grow by another 50 percent by 2050. By that time 85 percent of the world population will live in developing countries, where most of the projected growth will be taking place. In fact, according to the United Nations Population Fund,

"The 48 least-developed countries will nearly triple in size." Even in the United States, the population has increased by 70 million people just since 1970 (primarily along the coasts, where coincidentally the ecosystems are the most fragile). At 1 percent, the United States has the highest annual growth rate of any developed nation and could double its population within seventy-two years. . . .

Reducing Overpopulation by Addressing Women's Needs

Endemic poverty, low levels of education, and weak family planning programs contribute to a fertility rate of over six children per woman in poor regions of the world. Studies have shown that one-third of the population growth in the world is the result of incidental or unwanted pregnancy. Furthermore, over 600,000 women die every year because of complications from unwanted pregnancy and abortion—deaths that could have been avoided through family planning.

Unprotected intercourse results in not only pregnancy but disease for many women. There are an estimated 333 million new cases of sexually transmitted diseases (STDs) each year. Worldwide, the disease burden of STDs in women is more than five times that of men. Sadly, the total worldwide annual cost of better reproductive health care is about $17 billion—less than one week of the world's expenditures on armaments!

The United Nations is attempting to address these pressing issues, recommending the actions put forth by its 1994 International Conference on Population and Development in Cairo. These are universal access to reproductive health care, including voluntary family planning, by 2015; greater access to education for girls; and action to promote gender equality. Survey data suggest that some 120 million additional women worldwide would be using a modern family planning method if information and affordable services were easily available, and if their families and communities were more supportive.

We in the Western world tend to see information and support as givens. Many of us consider it incomprehensible that rational adults should choose to bring babies into lives that face the daily threat of starvation, and yet many men and women living in underdeveloped countries are unaware that they can do anything about controlling fertility. Traditional values and culturally reinforced gender inequality are powerful forces that keep people from being open to change. Religion plays a role as well.

It is apparent that women need to be brought into balance with men so that they have more and better opportunities for education, a greater voice in decisions that impact their lives, and more support. The first step in that transition is the transmission of truthful information. If women know where to go to get help, if they can become better informed about opportunities and services available, and if they pursue better schooling and find fulfilling employment, they may make life decisions that have a positive impact on the problem of overpopulation for years into the future. The World Population Fund estimates that the number of children in many developing countries would fall by a third if there were access to the kinds of services that people need.

Food and Water for the Billions of Us

If efforts at population control fail and we continue to grow dramatically as a species, we will find ourselves facing various shortages. Our supply of water for sustenance and for agricultural use, for example, will be drastically reduced. By the year 2025, the number of people living in either water-scarce or water-stressed conditions could quadruple to between 2.4 billion and 3.2 billion people, depending on future rates of population growth. Water shortages are likely to grow especially acute in the Middle East and in much of Africa.

For many people in the world, the overpopulation situation is already nearly impossible and getting worse. An esti-

Tom Toles. © 1994. Distributed by Universal Press Syndicate. Reproduced by permission.

mated 420 million people live today in countries that have less than 0.17 of an acre of cultivated land per person. (That figure is the estimated minimum parcel capable of supplying a vegetarian diet for one person without use of costly chemicals and fertilizers.) By 2025 the number of people living in such countries is expected to increase to between 557 million and 1.04 billion. As it is now, more than three billion people worldwide are suffering from malnutrition, according to the World Health Organization—the largest proportion of malnourished persons in history. Malnourishment compounds suffering because it makes already vulnerable humans more vulnerable to other diseases, such as diarrhea, malaria, and AIDS.

In contrast, a person living in a First World city requires the equivalent of about 11.1 acres of productive land for food, water, housing, and goods. As well-known population activists Paul and Ann Ehrlich note,

> Applying this "ecological footprint" standard to a city such as Sydney, Australia, shows that it would need an area of productive land 35 times as big as the city to sustain itself. For the projected world population in 2050 to live like people in Sydney, we'd need about 124 billion acres of productive land—around six times all the productive land on the planet.

It is astounding to realize how much of the world's productive land, not to mention natural resources in general, is necessary to sustain the way of life that developed countries are used to—while billions are hopelessly relegated to starvation. It is a complete impossibility to feed the entire world population in the manner to which First World countries have become accustomed. . . .

Reduction of Lifestyle

One would reason that the 18 million more people added to the world's population by India last year [2003] would make a far greater negative impact on the Earth than the 2.5 million added to the United States last year. If considered in light of sheer numbers, this would be true, of course. But when we consider the impact of each person's lifestyle and the resources used to sustain it, we reach an entirely different conclusion. Most of the 18 million newcomers to India will live in extreme poverty; not so the newcomers to the United States. Gregory Mankiw, Allie S. Freed Professor of Economics at Harvard University, points out how dramatically lifestyles in America differ from those in India (and elsewhere):

> Although Americans comprise only five percent of the world's population, we use 25 percent of its resources and produce more trash and pollution than citizens of most other nations. The average American's energy use is equiva-

> lent to the consumption of two Japanese, six Mexicans, 13 Chinese, 32 Indians, 140 Bangladeshis, 284 Tanzanians or 372 Ethiopians. Because Americans consume much more of the Earth's resources than do people in India, 2.5 million additional Americans have the environmental impact of nearly 80 million Indians. In this light, U.S. growth might be considered more costly to the planet than India's growth. . . .

Life in the Rats' Nest

In Mexico City, it actually snows fecal matter. Mexico City is the fourth most populated urban area in the world, at almost 20 million people. Tens of thousands of the city's residents live next to a trash dump or under a cardboard box, almost 10 percent of the population surviving on less than one U.S. dollar per day. With so many people having no sanitation facilities, their human waste dries, gets picked up by the wind, and then is breathed by everyone else.

In India, an American nun was riding on a train stuffed with people inside and out, with many riding and hanging on to the roof outside. While standing in the densely crowded aisle and trying to keep her balance, she suddenly felt pressure and saw that an apparently abandoned baby had been left on her arm. (Don't be tempted to assume that "it doesn't happen here." Approximately five thousand infants are abandoned in the United States each year.)

In Nepal, the farmers struggle to grow food wherever they can. In some places they grow it on three-foot-wide terraces, each terrace separated from the next by a ten-foot rise. The land is so steep that some of the precious topsoil washes away every time it rains. And despite the vanishing farmland, mothers in Nepal keep having babies a year or less apart. Of those babies, many die because there is not enough food for everyone.

In Malawi, villagers must now spend four hours doing a task that previously took only one hour. Having harvested too many trees without replanting, they must walk an hour and a half to a forest preserve each day, spend an hour looking for sufficient sticks of wood to cook their daily meal, and then walk back home again carrying the wood.

Given the prevalence of stories such as these, why is it that we have so much trouble making the connection between runaway population growth and environmental crises? "It seems plain that the issues that matter most to us—biodiversity, urban sprawl, loss of rainforests and old-growth trees, air and water pollution—have their roots in the incredibly successful propagation of the human species," writes Jim Motavalli in *E/The Environmental Magazine*. Success usually brings celebration and joy, but human overpopulation on Earth is bringing untold misery to most living things and threatening our very existence as a species.

And this is only one side of the problem—the human side. Over-population is profoundly impacting Earth's entire web of life. How will the stately and critically endangered tiger be able to peacefully coexist with humanity in modern India, whose population is expected to reach 1.5 billion and surpass China by 2050?

> *"For healthy ecosystems, we need large core areas, linkages between those core areas, and the presence of keystone species such as large carnivores."*

Connecting Large Wilderness Areas Will Help Conserve the Environment

Dave Foreman

Dave Foreman is a leading proponent of wilderness conservation and the author of several books, including Confessions of an Eco-Warrior *and* Rewilding North America. *Foreman argues in the following viewpoint that extinction is a serious problem, and that steps must be taken to preserve endangered species. He proposes that large wilderness areas be created by linking existing reserves and creating new ones in North America. Foreman believes that big carnivores, which require large habitats, keep ecosystems healthy.*

As you read, consider the following questions:

1. According to Foreman, how many extinction periods have biologists identified?

Dave Foreman, *Nature's Operating Instructions: The True Biotechnologies*, San Francisco, CA: Sierra Club Books, 2004.

2. How, as explained in this viewpoint, do coyotes help preserve songbirds?
3. What wild animals, according to the author, eat songbird eggs?

I believe that extinction is the main event going on in the world today. Since the dodo became extinct on an island in the Indian Ocean in the 1600s, we have seen dozens of species of birds and mammals disappear, and even more insects, plants, reptiles, and fish. We are living in an age of mass extinction.

In the five hundred million years since complex animals evolved, there have been five great extinction events that we have carefully identified through studying the fossil records. The last one was sixty-five million years ago, when the dinosaurs disappeared forever because a massive comet hit earth somewhere in the Gulf of Mexico. In the 1960s, wildlife biologists began to compare notes from all over the world. Spotted cats like the ocelot were fast disappearing. Reptiles like the desert tortoise were becoming endangered as their habitats were destroyed and they were run over by dirt bikes. We passed the Endangered Species Act to try to stem the tide of extinction, but it soon became obvious that we were seeing not just the loss of a few beautiful species like the ocelot and wonderful little critters like the desert tortoise. We were, in fact, in the middle of the sixth great extinction, the Pleistocene-Holocene event.

Leading biologists like E.O. Wilson have predicted that we could lose up to one-third of all species in the next fifty to a hundred years. This tragedy is a central reality of our time, and we cannot blame an asteroid for causing it. It has one and only one cause, and that is six billion human beings breeding, eating, manufacturing, warring, and traveling. We have become a plague of extraterrestrial proportions on the earth, and we are causing the extinction of many of our fellow travelers, including our closest relatives, the primates, and many other species.

Human-caused extinction takes five main forms. One is the direct persecution and killing of certain animals, such as the campaign we waged in the mid-twentieth century to wipe out all wolves in the United States, or the mass slaughter and poisoning of prairie dogs. Another is the introduction of exotic, invasive species, such as that of the bullfrog into southwestern streams, where it eats the native leopard frog and native fish. Disease is another major factor: exotic diseases are spread by humans, pets, rats, and domestic animals. The black-footed ferret was nearly wiped out by distemper, for example. Of course, pollution and industrial activities of all kinds pose a major threat to the survival of many species.

But the leading cause of extinction is habitat destruction through agriculture, overgrazing, development, mining, logging, and other fragmentation of the landscape. If you destroy habitat, you will lose species. A freeway is very difficult for even the wily coyote to get across.

The Importance of Large Animals

We know from studying island ecosystems that there is a direct relationship between the size of an island and the number of species it holds. As we break up habitat in smaller and smaller pieces, we see the number of species decline. Through careful scientific research we have determined that even Yellowstone National Park is not big enough in itself to maintain viable populations of wide-ranging species like grizzly bears, wolverines, and wolves. And through research in the tropics, oceans, and temperate areas we have recently learned just how important large carnivores are. For example, if you protect enough habitat for a healthy population of wolves, you are protecting habitat for many other species as well.

Top-down regulation is the key to maintaining ecosystems. On the Pacific coast, when sea otters are present, so are healthy kelp forests. When sea otters disappear, the kelp forests do too, because the sea otter's main prey, the sea urchin, is a voracious predator of kelp forests. When you remove the otters, sea urchin populations explode, destroying the kelp forests and the hundreds of species that depend on them.

In suburban San Diego, biologist Michael Soulé has shown what happens as suburbs surround remaining patches of coastal sage scrub in the canyons. As long as coyotes are present in the canyons, all the native birds are there. As soon as the coyotes disappear, so do the native birds. Why? Because any smart house cat, like my beautiful cat Chama, knows to stay home when coyotes are about. Remove the coyotes and the house cats, foxes, skunks, and possums become emboldened and go into these habitats and eat songbirds and their eggs.

Carnivores Help the Wild

The presence of large carnivores affects not just the presence of other species but, just as important, how they interact with their habitat. We have seen how the reintroduction of wolves has entirely changed the behavior of elk in Yellowstone National Park. No longer are elk loafing around and over-grazing meadows. The elk are suddenly elk again: they're looking over their shoulders, they're running around, and the land is much healthier for it. In Isle Royal National Park in Lake Superior, when there's a healthy and balanced population of wolves, they maintain an appropriately balanced population of moose, which means that the balsam fir forest is healthy. But if we remove the wolves or there are too few wolves, the moose overpopulate and overgraze, with dire consequences for the forest.

We have known for a long time that neotropical migrant songbirds of the eastern United States—the warblers and thrushes that go south in the winter and breed in North

America in the summer—are declining in numbers. Part of the reason is destruction of their habitat. But a major factor is the absence of mountain lions and wolves. Mountain lions and wolves don't eat baby songbirds. No self-respecting mountain lion is going to skulk about the forest for warbler eggs to suck. The problem is that there are no longer any mountain lions or wolves in the eastern forest, which means the smaller meso-predators multiply. Raccoons, who don't have the self-respect not to suck warbler eggs, become more abundant and act more boldly in the absence of predators. They, along with skunks and foxes, go into the forest and eat songbird eggs and baby warblers.

All over the world we are finding that when we remove large carnivores, the whole system begins to unravel. Large carnivores need big core habitats and they need connections between them. For example, a huge human-made reservoir in Venezuela created a number of islands that are too small to support populations of jaguars and harpy eagles. In the absence of these predators, leaf-eating monkeys and other small animals have become unnaturally abundant, changing the entire composition of the forest. Now only five species of trees are reproducing in a forest that once had sixty.

In the United States, we simply no longer have wild areas large enough to maintain habitat for large populations of jaguars, grizzlies, or wolves. What we need to do is to link wildlands together so that animals can disperse. All it takes to keep two geographically separated populations of mountain lions connected and to avoid inbreeding is for a horny adolescent male mountain lion to range between the two every ten years or so.

Rewilding

This recognition leads me to the idea of rewilding. For healthy ecosystems, we need large core areas, linkages between those core areas, and the presence of keystone species such as large

Mega Links Are the Key to Rewilding North America

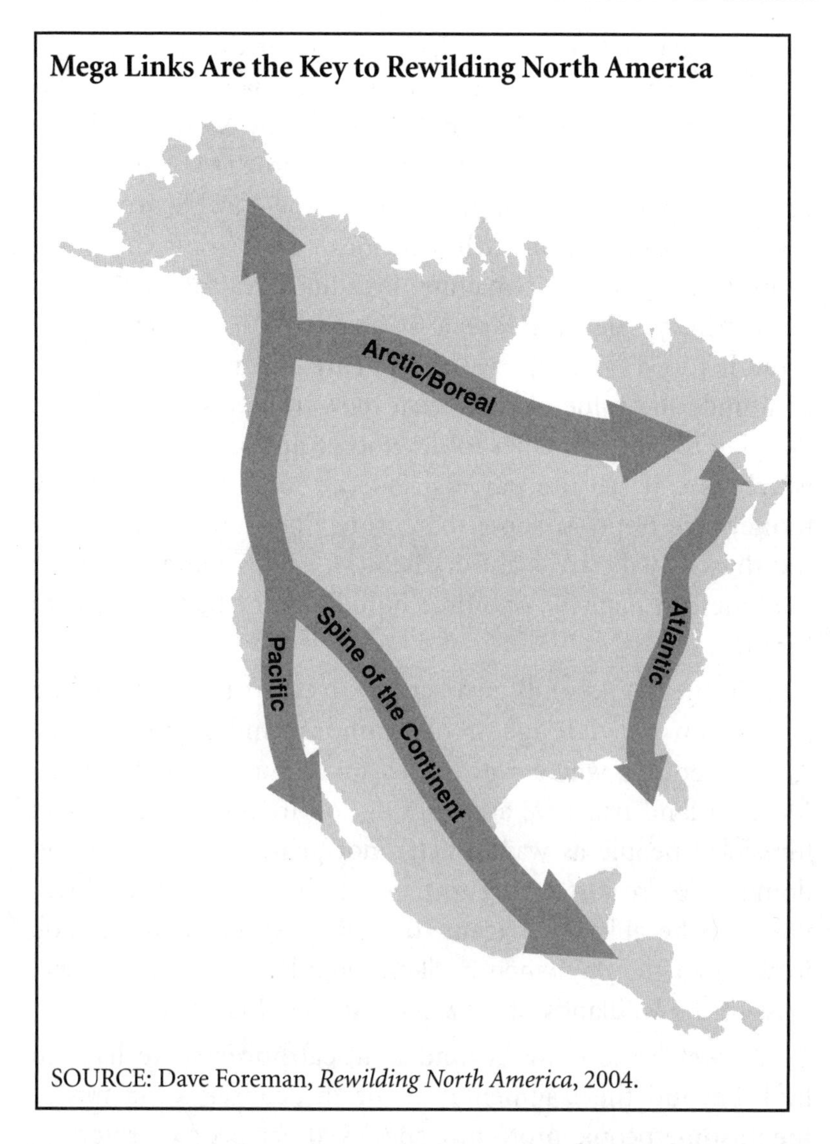

SOURCE: Dave Foreman, *Rewilding North America*, 2004.

carnivores. How do we achieve this? The Wildlands Project and its sister magazine *Wild Earth* are exploring how we might create such areas, link them, and reintroduce large carnivores to restore healthy landscapes.

To do our work, we have to look across national borders and across the borders between public and private land. Jaguars and thick-billed parrots are both native to New Mexico and Arizona, but they were driven south of the U.S. border a hundred years ago. If we are going to get jaguars and thick-billed parrots back in the mountains of New Mexico and Arizona, we have to protect their habitat in northern Mexico. Recently the Wildlands Project and its partners in Mexico signed a groundbreaking deal with a Mexican land grant commune to protect the largest remaining breeding area for thick-billed parrots in the Sierra Madre, a six-thousand-acre patch of old-growth forest. Because we are paying the members of the commune the value of the forest, they are not going to log it. We plan to work together to develop ecotourism, so that bird-watchers can see the parrots and the local folks can make money. We hope to show that protecting nature, protecting the thick-billed parrot and its habitat, brings more money in the long run than the one-time liquidation of that old-growth forest.

Another Wildlands project revolves around a breeding population of wild jaguars one hundred miles south of the Arizona border, where ranches sell for $15 an acre. Through a Mexican land trust, we are working to buy those ranches and hire local people as wardens. It's not gringos coming in and doing it. We're just trying to provide the money so that jaguars will be able once again to freely disperse, and we look forward to the day when a viable population of jaguars will exist in the wildlands of Arizona and New Mexico.

As well as looking beyond political borders, we have to look beyond the fragmentation of the conservation movement: some people protecting species, other people protecting land, others working on economic incentives. We have to bring it all together in a single, reasonable, coordinated effort to break down barriers and rebuild wild nature in North America, so that human civilization and society can once again begin to coexist with the wild.

I believe that's the fundamental challenge of our times. Do we have the generosity of spirit and the greatness of heart to allow some land a will of its own, where we are not dominating, controlling, and manipulating everything, where some things are beyond human control? That is the other great value of large carnivores to the human spirit: they teach us humility, a virtue in short supply. We are surrounded by human arrogance, but there is nothing like comparing your tracks to a grizzly bear's to teach you humility, to show us that we are not gods upon the planet, lords of all that we survey.

> *"In recent years, there has been a dramatic rise in ecologically oriented design practices and projects."*

America Should Design Products that Benefit the Environment

Fritjof Capra

Fritjof Capra is the author of several international best-selling books, including The Tao of Physics, *and is the founder of the Center for Ecoliteracy in Berkeley, California. In the following viewpoint Capra claims that ecological design can help conserve the environment. Ecologically designed products, contends Capra, imitate nature so as to augment rather than damage the environment. Capra, for instance, contends that industrial processes can be changed so that any wastes produced in the manufacture of one product can be used in the production of another.*

As you read, consider the following questions:

1. According to Capra, what is the first step in ecological design?
2. In this viewpoint, what is an example of ecological design?

Fritjof Capra, "Eco Literacy," *Adbusters*, vol. 13, January-February 2005. Reproduced by permission.

3. What types of activity does the author propose should be taxed?

The great challenge of our time is to create sustainable communities—communities designed in such a manner that their ways of life, technologies and social institutions honor, support, and cooperate with nature's inherent ability to sustain life. We do not need to invent them from scratch but can model them after nature's ecosystems, sustainable communities of plants, animals and microorganisms.

Ecoliteracy

The first step in this endeavor must be to become "ecologically literate," i.e., to understand the principles of organization that ecosystems have evolved to sustain the web of life. In the coming decades the survival of humanity will depend on our ecological literacy—our ability to understand the basic principles of ecology and to live accordingly. Ecological literacy, or "ecoliteracy," must become a critical skill for politicians, business leaders, and professionals in all spheres, and should be the most important part of education at all levels—from primary and secondary schools to colleges, universities, and the continuing education and training of professionals.

We need to teach our children (and our political and corporate leaders!) the fundamental facts of life—that one species' waste is another species' food; that matter cycles continually through the web of life; that the energy driving the ecological cycles flows from the sun; that diversity assures resilience; that life, from its beginning more than three billion years ago, did not take over the planet by combat but by networking.

Ecodesign

Ecoliteracy is the first step. The second is ecodesign. We need to apply our ecological knowledge to the fundamental rede-

The Sustainable Society

A sustainable society is one that has in place informational, social, and institutional mechanisms to keep in check the positive feedback loops that cause exponential population and capital growth. This means that birth rates roughly equal death rates, and investment rates roughly equal depredation rates, unless or until technical changes and social decisions justify a considered, limited change in the levels of population or capital. In order to be socially sustainable, the combination of population and capital and technology would have to be configured so that the material living standard is adequate and secure for everyone and fairly distributed. To be materially and energetically sustainable, the economy's throughputs would have to meet Herman Daly's three conditions:

- Its rates of use of renewable resources do not exceed their rates of regeneration.
- Its rates of use of nonrenewable resources do not exceed the rate at which sustainable renewable substitutes are developed.
- Its rates of pollution emission do not exceed the assimilative capacity of the environment.

Donella Meadows, Limits to Growth, *2004.*

sign of our technologies and social institutions, so as to bridge the current gap between human design and the ecologically sustainable systems of nature.

Following environmental educator David Orr, I have come to adopt an ecological definition of design as "the shaping of flows of energy and matter for human purposes." Ecodesign is a process in which our human purposes are carefully meshed with the larger patterns and flows of the natural world. Ecodesign principles reflect the principles of organization that nature has evolved to sustain the web of life. To practice design in such a context requires a fundamental shift in our attitude toward nature, a shift from finding out what we can extract from nature, to what we can learn.

In recent years, there has been a dramatic rise in ecologically oriented design practices and projects. They include a worldwide renaissance in organic farming, involving technologies based on ecological knowledge rather than chemistry or genetic engineering to increase yields, control pests, and build soil fertility; the organization of different industries into ecological clusters, in which the waste of any one organization is a resource for another; the shift from a product-oriented economy to a "service-and-flow" economy, in which industrial raw materials and technical components cycle continually between manufacturers and users; buildings designed to produce more energy than they use, emit no waste, and monitor their own performance; hybrid-electric cars achieving fuel efficiencies of 60 miles per gallon and more; and the development of efficient hydrogen fuel cells that promise to inaugurate a new era in energy production—the "hydrogen economy." These technologies and projects all incorporate the basic principles of ecology, and thus tend to be small-scale that are diverse, energy efficient, non-polluting, community-oriented, and labor intensive.

Institutional Change

To implement these technologies effectively we will also need to redesign many of our social institutions. For example, we need to change our tax system from taxing the things we value—jobs, savings, investments—to taxing the things we recognize as harmful, like pollution and resource depletion.

We need to end the numerous perverse subsidies of unsustainable and harmful industries and corporate practices. We must recognize that unlimited economic growth can only lead to disaster, and we need to reorganize our economies accordingly.

The technologies available today provide compelling evidence that the transition to a sustainable future is no longer a technical nor a conceptual problem. It is a problem of values and political will.

VIEWPOINT 

"U.S. factory farms generated 1.4 billion tons of animal waste in 1996, which . . . pollutes American waterways more than all other industrial sources combined."

Reducing Meat Consumption Will Help Conserve the Environment

Jim Motavalli

Jim Motavalli is a journalist and editor of E/The Environmental Magazine. *Motavalli argues in the following viewpoint that reducing the consumption of meat would benefit the environment. He contends that the production of meat products adversely affects the environment due to its intensive use of energy and resources, the dumping of animal waste products into waterways, and accidental spills from factory farms.*

As you read, consider the following questions:

1. According to this viewpoint, how many head of livestock are currently being farmed worldwide?

Jim Motavalli, "The Case Against Meat," *E/The Environmental Magazine*, vol. 13, January-February 2002.

2. What fraction of raw materials and fossil fuels are consumed by animal production in the United States, as cited by Motavalli?
3. Organic products accounted for what dollar amount of sales in 1999, according to this viewpoint?

There has never been a better time for environmentalists to become vegetarians. Evidence of the environmental impacts of a meat-based diet is piling up at the same time its health effects are becoming better known. Meanwhile, full-scale industrialized factory farming—which allows diseases to spread quickly as animals are raised in close confinement—has given rise to recent, highly publicized epidemics of meat-borne illnesses. At presstime [January 2002], the first discovery of mad cow disease in a Tokyo suburb caused beef prices to plummet in Japan and many people to stop eating meat.

All this comes at a time when meat consumption is reaching an all-time high around the world, quadrupling in the last 50 years. There are 20 billion head of livestock taking up space on the Earth, more than triple the number of people. According to the Worldwatch Institute, global livestock population has increased 60 percent since 1961, and the number of fowl being raised for human dinner tables has nearly quadrupled in the same time period, from 4.2 billion to 15.7 billion. U.S. beef and pork consumption has tripled since 1970, during which time it has more than doubled in Asia.

One reason for the increase in meat consumption is the rise of fast-food restaurants as an American dietary staple. As Eric Schlosser noted in his best-selling book *Fast Food Nation*, "Americans now spend more money on fast food—$110 billion a year—than they do on higher education. They spend more on fast food than on movies, books, magazines, newspapers, videos and recorded music—combined."

Strong growth in meat production and consumption continues despite mounting evidence that meat-based diets are unhealthy, and that just about every aspect of meat production—from grazing-related loss of cropland and open space, to the inefficiencies of feeding vast quantities of water and grain to cattle in a hungry world, to pollution from "factory farms"—is an environmental disaster with wide and sometimes catastrophic consequences. Oregon State University agriculture professor Peter Cheeke calls factory farming "a frontal assault on the environment, with massive groundwater and air pollution problems."

World Hunger and Resources

The 4.8 pounds of grain fed to cattle to produce one pound of beef for human beings represents a colossal waste of resources in a world still teeming with people who suffer from profound hunger and malnutrition.

According to the British group Vegfam, a 10-acre farm can support 60 people growing soybeans, 24 people growing wheat, 10 people growing corn and only two producing cattle. Britain—with 56 million people—could support a population of 250 million on an all-vegetable diet. Because 90 percent of U.S. and European meat eaters' grain consumption is indirect (first being fed to animals), westerners each consume 2,000 pounds of grain a year. Most grain in underdeveloped countries is consumed directly.

While it is true that many animals graze on land that would be unsuitable for cultivation, the demand for meat has taken millions of productive acres away from farm inventories. The cost of that is incalculable. As *Diet For a Small Planet* author Frances Moore Lappé writes, imagine sitting down to an eight-ounce steak. "Then imagine the room filled with 45 to 50 people with empty bowls in front of them. For the 'feed cost' of your steak, each of their bowls could be filled with a full cup of cooked cereal grains."

Harvard nutritionist Jean Mayer estimates that reducing meat production by just 10 percent in the U.S. would free

A Positive Lifestyle Change

When we dare to think of the environmental threats facing our planet, we must indeed consider a complex web of interrelated problems: air pollution, water pollution, land contamination, soil erosion, wildlife loss, desertification (the turning of verdant land into a condition resembling natural desert), rain forest destruction, and global warming. Humankind's profligate consumption of animal products has made a significant contribution to all of these ills, and it stands as the leading cause of many of them. Certainly these problems wouldn't disappear overnight if the world suddenly became vegetarian, but no other lifestyle change could produce as positive an impact on these profound threats to our collective survival as the adoption of a plant-based diet.

Howard F. Lyman, Mad Cowboy, *1998.*

enough grain to feed 60 million people. Authors Paul and Anne Ehrlich note that a pound of wheat can be grown with 60 pounds of water, whereas a pound of meat requires 2,500 to 6,000 pounds.

Environmental Costs

Energy intensive U.S. factory farms generated 1.4 billion tons of animal waste in 1996, which, the Environmental Protection Agency reports, pollutes American waterways more than all other industrial sources combined. Meat production has also been linked to severe erosion of billions of acres of once-productive farmland and to the destruction of rainforests.

McDonald's took a group of British animal rights activists to court in the 1990s because they had linked the fast food giant to an unhealthy diet and rainforest destruction. The defendants, who fought the company to a standstill, made a convincing case. In court documents, the activists asserted, "From 1970 onwards, beef from cattle reared on ex-rainforest land was supplied to McDonald's." In a policy statement, McDonald's claims that it "does not purchase beef which threatens tropical rainforests anywhere in the world," but it does not deny past purchases.

According to People for the Ethical Treatment of Animals (PETA), livestock raised for food produce 130 times the excrement of the human population, some 87,000 pounds per second. The Union of Concerned Scientists points out that 20 tons of livestock manure is produced annually for every U.S. household. The much-publicized 1989 *Exxon Valdez* oil spill in Alaska dumped 12 million gallons of oil into Prince William Sound, but the relatively unknown 1995 New River hog waste spill in North Carolina poured 25 million gallons of excrement and urine into the water, killing an estimated 10 to 14 million fish and closing 364,000 acres of coastal shellfishing beds. Hog waste spills have caused the rapid spread of a virulent microbe called *Pfiesteria piscicida,* which has killed a billion fish in North Carolina alone.

More than a third of all raw materials and fossil fuels consumed in the U.S. are used in animal production. Beef production alone uses more water than is consumed in growing the nation's entire fruit and vegetable crop. Producing a single hamburger patty uses enough fuel to drive 20 miles and causes the loss of five times its weight in topsoil. In his book *The Food Revolution*, author John Robbins estimates that "you'd save more water by not eating a pound of California beef than you would by not showering for an entire year." Because of deforestation to create grazing land, each vegetarian saves an acre of trees per year.

"We definitely take up more environmental space when we eat meat," says Barbara Bramble of the National Wildlife Federation. "I think it's consistent with environmental values to eat lower on the food chain." . . .

The Vegetarian Solution

Vegetarianism is not a new phenomenon. The ancient Greek philosopher Pythagoras was vegetarian, and until the mid-19th century, people who abstained from meat were known as "Pythagoreans." Famous followers of Pythagoras' diet included Leonardo da Vinci, Benjamin Franklin, George Bernard Shaw and Albert Einstein. The word "vegetarian" was coined in 1847 to give a name to what was then a tiny movement in England.

In the U.S., the 1971 publication of *Diet For a Small Planet* was a major catalyst for introducing people to a healthy vegetarian diet. Other stimuli included Peter Singer's 1975 book *Animal Liberation*, which gave vegetarianism a moral underpinning; Singer and Jim Mason's book *Animal Factories*, the first exposé of confinement agriculture; and John Robbins' 1987 *Diet for a New America*. In the U.S., according to a 1998 *Vegetarian Journal* survey, 82 percent of vegetarians are motivated by health concerns, 75 percent by ethics, the environment and/or animal rights, 31 percent because of taste and 26 percent because of economics. . . .

How many vegetarians are there in the U.S.? It depends on whom you ask. A PETA fact sheet asserts that 12 million Americans are vegetarians, and 19,000 make the switch every week. Pamela Rice, author of *101 Reasons Why I'm a Vegetarian*, puts the number at 4.5 million, or 2.5 percent of the population, based on recent surveys. Older counts, from 1992, put the number of people who "consider themselves" to be vegetarians at seven percent of the U.S. population, or an impressive 18 million. A 1991 Gallup Poll indicated that 20 percent of the population look for vegetarian menu items when they eat out.

Actual vegetarian numbers may be lower. VRG got virtually the same results in two separate Roper Polls it sponsored in 1994 and 1997: One percent of the public, or between two and three million, is vegetarian (eats no meat or fish, but may eat dairy and/or eggs), with a third to half of them living on a vegan diet (eschewing all animal products). Roughly five percent in both studies "never eat red meat." A 2000 poll was slightly more optimistic, putting the number of vegetarians at 2.5 percent of the population. Women are more likely to be vegetarians than men; and—surprisingly—Republicans are slightly more likely to abstain from meat than Democrats.

The American Dietetic Association says in a position statement, "Appropriately planned vegetarian diets are healthful, are nutritionally adequate and provide health benefits in the prevention and treatment of certain diseases." Vegetarians now have excellent opportunities to put together well-planned meals. The sale of organic products in natural food stores is the highest growth niche in the food industry, according to *Nutrition Business Journal,* and it grew 22 percent in 1999 to $4 billion. The natural food markets of today are not the tiny storefronts of yesteryear, but full-service supermarkets, with vigorous competition among giant national chains. Diverse veggie entrees are now available in most supermarkets and on a growing list of restaurant menus.

> *"The goal of tax restructuring is to get the market to tell the ecological truth."*

Products That Harm the Environment Should Be Taxed More Heavily

Bernie Fischlowitz-Roberts

Writer Bernie Fischlowitz-Roberts specializes in green taxes, solar cell products, and green power at the Earth Policy Institute. In the following viewpoint Fischlowitz-Roberts argues that governments should raise taxes on environmentally destructive products and activities, and lower them on income and other things of value. The author points to several European countries that have used tax shifting as evidence that this type of restructuring benefits the environment. For example, when gasoline is taxed at a higher rate, consumers drive less, thereby cutting greenhouse gas emissions.

As you read, consider the following questions:

1. What percentage of worldwide tax revenues has tax shifting accounted for, according to this viewpoint?

Bernie Fischlowitz-Roberts, *The Earth Policy Reader,* Washington, D.C.: W.W. Norton and Company, 2002.

2. Carbon emissions have been reduced by what percentage in Finland due to tax shifting, as detailed by the author?
3. What amount of government subsidies are given to environmentally destructive activities worldwide each year, according to Fischlowitz-Roberts?

Many countries have implemented taxes on environmentally destructive products and activities while simultaneously reducing taxes on social security contributions or income. The scale of tax shifting has been relatively small thus far, accounting for only 3 percent of tax revenues worldwide. It is increasingly clear, however, that countries are recognizing the power of tax systems not only for raising revenue, but also for shaping economic decisions of individuals and businesses. The German tax shift, one of the most advanced to date, illustrates how countries are modifying tax systems to reach environmental and economic objectives.

Germany has implemented environmental tax reform in several stages by lowering income taxes and raising energy taxes. In 1999, taxes on gasoline, heating oils, and natural gas were increased, and a new tax on electricity was adopted. This revenue was used to decrease employer and employee contributions to the pension fund. Energy tax rises for many energy-intensive industries were substantially lower, however, reflecting concerns about international competitiveness.

The second stage, which began in 2000, involved further reductions in payroll taxes and increases on those on motor fuels and electricity. Germany has shifted 2 percent of its tax burden from incomes to environmentally destructive activities. As a result, fuel sales were 5 percent lower in the first half of 2001 than in the same period in 1999. Consumption of gasoline decreased by 12 percent over the same time, and carpool agencies reported growth of 25 percent in the first half of 2000.

Though Chancellor Gerhard Schroeder, concerned about the September 2002 elections, . . . prevented any additional energy tax increases until 2003, his main opponent, Edward Stoiber, has pledged to continue with environmental tax reforms if elected. The agreement of Schroeder and Stoiber on the need to continue the tax shift is encouraging.

Taxing Bad Business

The idea behind tax shifting is that raising taxes on products and activities that society wishes to discourage will encourage more environmentally friendly ways of doing business. For example, one part of the United Kingdom's environmental tax reform involved a steadily increasing fuel tax known as a fuel duty escalator, which was in effect from 1993 until 1999. As a result, fuel consumption from road transportation dropped, and the average fuel efficiency of trucks over 33 tons increased by 13 percent between 1993 and 1998. Ultra-low sulfur diesel had a lower tax rate than regular diesel, which caused its share of domestic diesel sales to jump from 5 percent in July 1998 to 43 percent in February 1999; by the end of 1999, the nation had completely converted to ultra-low sulfur diesel.

The Netherlands has also implemented a series of environmental tax shifts. A general fuel tax, originally implemented in 1988 and modified in 1992, is levied on fossil fuels; the rates are based on both the carbon and the energy contents of the fuel. Between 1996 and 1998, a Regulatory Energy Tax (RET) was implemented, which taxed natural gas, electricity, fuel oil, and heating oil. Unlike the fuel tax, which was designed principally for revenue generation, the RET's goal was to change behaviors by creating incentives for energy efficiency. To maintain competitiveness, major energy users were exempted from the taxes, so this tax fell mainly on individuals.

Since 60 percent of the revenue from these Dutch taxes came from households, the taxes were offset by decreasing income taxes. The 40 percent of revenue derived from businesses was recycled through three mechanisms: a reduction in employer contributions to social security, a reduction in corporate income taxes, and an increased tax exemption for self-employed people. This tax shift has caused household energy costs to increase, which has resulted in a 15-percent reduction in consumer electricity use and a 5- to 10-percent decrease in fuel usage.

Finland first implemented a carbon dioxide (CO_2) tax in 1990. Between 1990 and 1998, the country's CO_2 emissions decreased by almost 7 percent. Finland's environmental taxes, like those in most countries, are far from uniform: the electricity tax is greater for households and the service sector than for industry.

Sweden's experiment with tax shifting began in 1991, when it raised taxes on carbon and sulfur emissions and reduced income taxes. Manufacturing industries received exemptions and rebates from many of the environmental taxes, and as a result their tax rates were only half of those paid by households. In 2001, the government increased taxes on diesel fuel, heating oil, and electricity while lowering income taxes and social security contributions. Six percent of all government revenue in Sweden has now been shifted. This has helped Sweden reduce greenhouse gas emissions more quickly than anticipated. A political agreement between the government and the opposition required a 4-percent reduction below 1990 levels by 2012. Yet by 2000, emissions were already down 3.9 percent from 1990—in large measure due to energy taxes.

A preliminary assessment of existing environmental tax shifts yields mixed results. Emissions of some taxed pollutants have decreased: some have declined absolutely, while others are lower than projected but still higher in absolute terms due to increased consumption associated with economic growth. Using price mechanisms to spur changes in consumer and producer behavior can work, but if tax rates are set too low they will not have the desired effect. The myriad exemptions given to industries, especially energy-intensive ones, in existing tax shift programs slow the restructuring. These exemp-

Creating an Honest Market

The key to restructuring the economy is the creation of an honest market, one that tells the ecological truth. The market is an incredible institution—with some remarkable strengths and some glaring weaknesses. It allocates scarce resources with an efficiency that no central planning body can match. It easily balances supply and demand and it sets prices that readily reflect both scarcity and abundance. The market does, however, have three fundamental weaknesses. It does not incorporate the indirect costs of providing goods or services into prices, it does not value nature's services properly, and it does not respect the sustainable-yield thresholds of natural systems such as fisheries, forests, rangelands, and aquifers.

Lester R. Brown, Plan B: Rescuing a Planet under Stress and a Civilization in Trouble, *2003.*

tions, created out of legitimate competitiveness concerns, nonetheless slow the creation of a more effective tax system.

Other Policy Measures

A number of complementary policy measures can help make environmental tax shifts more effective. First, eliminating subsidies to environmentally destructive industries will help the market send the right signals. Worldwide, environmentally destructive subsidies exceed $500 billion annually. As long as government subsidies encourage activities that the taxes seek to discourage, the effectiveness of tax shifting will be limited.

Second, tax harmonization within the European Union, where countries can agree on a framework of environmental tax shifts, might lessen the need for the numerous exemptions for industry that currently plague national environmental tax regimes. Even without harmonization, using border tax adjustments—where companies have environmental taxes rebated to them upon export and have domestic environmental taxes added to imports—can ensure international competitiveness.

Third, when trying to guarantee equitable results of tax shifting, opting for tax refunds for lower-income citizens rather than tax exemptions preserves the incentive effect of the environmental tax. Fourth, for items whose demand does not change appreciably with small changes in price, making tax rates substantially higher—in a predictable and transparent way—will decrease consumption more than many of the limited efforts to date. Finally, expanding the tax base to encompass more products and services with deleterious environmental impacts would greatly enhance the effectiveness of tax shifting.

Aviation fuel, for example, is currently tax-free worldwide, despite causing 3.5 percent of global warming. However, recent European discussions of imposing taxes on jet fuel are a promising development that might slow the projected growth in worldwide consumption by reducing air travel or by producing efficiency improvements that lower jet fuel consumption. Sweden's tax on domestic air transport, for example, prompted the one domestic airline at the time to alter the engines of its Fokker aircraft, which lowered hydrocarbon emissions by 90 percent.

If properly constructed, tax shifts can help make markets work more effectively by incorporating more of the indirect costs of goods and services into their prices and by changing consumer and producer behavior accordingly. The emergence of a world-leading wind turbine industry in Denmark, for example, is one result of Danish taxes on fossil fuels and electricity, which are among the highest in the world. These measures have also spurred sales of energy-efficient appliances and encouraged other energy-saving behavior.

The goal of tax restructuring is to get the market to tell the ecological truth. Thus far, tax shifts have been modest in scope and have produced positive, if modest, results. Creation of an eco-economy calls for tax shifts of much larger magnitude in order for prices to reflect their full costs and to produce the requisite changes in individual and collective behavior.

Periodical Bibliography

The following articles have been selected to supplement the diverse views presented in this chapter.

Liz Borkowski	"Sustainable Transportation," *Co-op America Quarterly*, Fall 2004.
H. Sterling Burnett	"Protecting the Environment Through the Ownership Society," *NCPA Studies*, January 25, 2006. www.ncpa.org.
Emily Green	"Organic Farms Viable Despite Lower Yields, Study Finds," *Los Angeles Times*, May 31, 2002.
Elizabeth Grossman	"Hi-Tech Wasteland," *Orion*, July/August 2004.
Robert Hinkley	"Redesigning Corporate Law," *Resurgence*, July/August 2002.
Francesca Lyman	"The New City Beautiful," *Yes*, Summer 2005.
David W. Orr	"Law of the Land," *Orion*, January/February 2004.
Randal O'Toole	"Are We Paving Paradise?" *Reason Policy Brief*, January 2004. www.reason.org.
Stuart L. Pimm and Clinton Jenkins	"Sustaining the Variety of Life," *Scientific American*, September 2005.
Bruce Sterling	"Can Technology Save the Planet," *Sierra*, July/August 2005.
Chris Strohm and Tracy F. Rysavy	"Good Food: The Joy, Health, and Security of It," *Co-op America Quarterly*, Summer 2003.

For Further Discussion

Chapter 1

1. Kenny Ausubel contends that to fix the world's environmental problems requires a concerted effort by governments. Joseph Bast, on the other hand, argues that what is needed for the environment is less government intervention rather than more. List the solutions that each author suggests for conserving the environment. Whose suggestions do you think would be more effective? Why? In general, do you think that government regulations are needed to conserve the environment? Or do you think people will better conserve the environment when such laws are eliminated? Explain.
2. Ross Gelbspan argues that global warming poses a serious threat to human societies, while Sallie Baliunas downplays the threat of global warming. Outline the main points that Gelbspan uses to support his claim. Then outline the responses that Baliunas makes for each of Gelbspan's points. In your opinion, who has the stronger argument and why?
3. Authors Derrick Jensen and George Draffan present a different view of the state of the world's forests than does Bjørn Lomborg. How does Jensen and Draffan's idea of what constitutes a forest differ from Lomborg's concept of a forest? How does this difference affect the data that the authors use to support their arguments?

Chapter 2

1. Guy Dauncey argues that renewable energy could supply a significant portion of America's energy needs. Jerry Taylor and Peter VanDoren, however, contend that fossil fuels

will continue to be the best choice for energy in the near future. Examine Dauncey's argument and list any assumptions that he makes when analyzing the energy market. In your opinion, are these assumptions reasonable? Then examine Taylor and VanDoren's argument and list their reasons why renewable energy is not a viable future energy option. Which energy plan would you choose and why?

2. Helen Caldicott contends that nuclear energy presents waste disposal problems and threatens human health, while John Ritch claims that nuclear energy is safe and waste disposal is not a problem. After reading these viewpoints, do you think that nuclear power should be expanded, reduced, or maintained at current levels? Explain your answer, citing from the viewpoints.
3. Jim Motavalli is optimistic about the growth of wind energy, while H. Sterling Burnett notes the environmental costs of wind power. According to these viewpoints, why do new wind energy projects often need the help of government programs? What kinds of government programs assist wind development? Do you think that the government should assist with the building of wind power plants? Why or why not?
4. Lester R. Brown claims that actions to reduce carbon emissions would be good for the economy whereas S. Fred Singer believes that doing so would harm the economy. What effects do you think laws intended to reduce greenhouse gases, which may reduce overall energy use, would have on people's lives in the United States? How would they affect the economy? How would they affect the environment? Do you think the United States was correct in not signing the Kyoto Protocol on carbon emissions? Explain.

Chapter 3

1. Roger Di Silvestro claims that the current Endangered Species Act has helped save endangered wildlife, while Nancy Marano and Ben Lieberman argue that the law interferes with property rights and should be changed. Do you believe that it is more important to protect endangered species, or should peoples' economic needs take precedence? Explain your answer.
2. The Natural Resources Defense Council would like to keep the Arctic National Wildlife Refuge protected from development, while Paul Driessen argues that America needs the oil in the refuge. Considering the arguments in each viewpoint, do you believe that oil drilling in the area is possible without harming the wildlife? Do you think it is important to have wilderness areas that are preserved from human development? Explain your answer, citing from the viewpoints.
3. Jonathan Rauch is optimistic about the development of genetically engineered crops, while Christopher D. Cook argues that industrial farming damages the environment due to the use of chemicals. What are Rauch's main arguments for the use of biotech crops? What evidence does Cook give that industrial farming is harming the environment? Considering the arguments in these viewpoints, do you think that the use of genetically modified crops is good for the environment? Why or why not?

Chapter 4

1. Dave Foreman proposes the creation of large, connected wilderness areas to help preserve wildlife. Do you think that the preservation of large carnivores such as grizzly bears, wolves, and mountain lions is important? Should more land in the United States be protected as wilderness areas? Explain your answers.

2. Ed McGaa believes that human overpopulation is at the root of environmental problems. What evidence does McGaa adduce to support his argument that human overpopulation is an environmental problem? What solutions for reducing population growth does McGaa discuss? Do you think any of these solutions are worthwhile? If so, which one(s) and why?
3. Fritjof Capra believes that our society could benefit from designing things with ecological processes in mind. Do you think that Capra's ideas are useful? Explain.
4. Jim Motavalli argues that the production of meat takes a large toll on the environment. Describe the evidence that he presents to support his argument. In your opinion, what is his most persuasive point and why?
5. Bernie Fischlowitz-Roberts believes that the government can help conserve the environment though the use of tax-shifting policies. List the evidence that she gives to support her argument. Do you think that tax shifting would work in the United States? Why or why not?

Organizations to Contact

Cato Institute
1000 Massachusetts Ave. NW, Washington, DC 20001-5403
(202) 842-0200 • fax: (202) 842-3490
e-mail: cato@cato.org
Web site: www.cato.org

The Cato Institute is a libertarian public policy research foundation that aims to limit the role of government and protect civil liberties. The institute believes Environmental Protection Agency regulations are too stringent. Publications offered on the Cato Web site include the bimonthly *Cato Policy Report*, the quarterly journal *Regulation*, the paper "The EPA's Clear Air-ogance," and the book *Climate of Fear: Why We Shouldn't Worry About Global Warming.*

Competitive Enterprise Institute (CEI)
1001 Connecticut Ave. NW, Ste. 1250
Washington, DC 20036
(202) 331-1010 • fax: (202) 331-0640
e-mail: info@cei.org
Web site: www.cei.org

CEI is a nonprofit public policy organization dedicated to the principles of free enterprise and limited government. The institute believes private incentives and property rights, rather than government regulations, are the best way to protect the environment. CEI's publications include the newsletter *Monthly Planet* (formerly *CEI Update*), On Point policy briefs, and the books *Global Warming and Other Eco-Myths* and *The True State of the Planet.*

Environmental Defense Fund (EDF)
257 Park Ave. South, New York, NY 10010
(212) 505-2100 • fax: (212) 505-0892
Web site: www.edf.org

The fund is a public interest organization of lawyers, scientists, and economists dedicated to the protection and improvement of environmental quality and public health. It publishes the bimonthly *EDF Letter.*

Environmental Protection Agency (EPA)
Ariel Rios Bldg., 1200 Pennsylvania Ave. NW
Washington, DC 20460
(202) 272-0167
Web site: www.epa.gov

The EPA is the federal agency in charge of protecting the environment and controlling pollution. The agency works toward these goals by enacting and enforcing regulations, identifying and fining polluters, assisting businesses and local environmental agencies, and cleaning up polluted sites. The EPA publishes periodic reports and the monthly *EPA Activities Update.*

Greenpeace USA
1436 U St. NW, Washington, DC 20009
(800) 326-0959 • fax: (202) 462-4507
Web site: www.greenpeace.org

Greenpeace supports wildlife preservation and opposes nuclear energy and the use of toxic chemicals. It uses direct-action techniques and strives for media coverage of its actions in an effort to educate the public. It publishes the quarterly magazine *Greenpeace.*

The Heritage Foundation
214 Massachusetts Ave. NE, Washington, DC 20002
(800) 544-4843 • fax: (202) 544-2260

e-mail: pubs@heritage.org
Web site: www.heritage.org

The Heritage Foundation is a conservative think tank that supports the principles of free enterprise and limited government in environmental matters. Its many publications include the following position papers: "Can No One Stop the EPA?" "How to Talk About Property Rights: Why Protecting Property Rights Benefits All Americans," and "How to Help the Environment Without Destroying Jobs."

National Audubon Society
700 Broadway, New York, NY 10003
(212) 979-3000 • fax: (212) 979-3188
e-mail: webmaster@list.audubon.org
Web site: www.audubon.org

The society seeks to conserve and restore natural ecosystems, focusing on birds and other wildlife, for the benefit of humanity and Earth's biological diversity. It publishes *Audubon* magazine and the *WatchList*, which identifies North American bird species that are at risk of becoming endangered.

National Wildlife Federation
11100 Wildlife Center Dr., Reston, VA 20190-5362
(800) 822-9919
Web site: www.nwf.org

The National Wildlife Federation is a nonprofit organization dedicated to preserving America's wildlife for future generations. It consists of members, volunteers, and affiliated organizations that work to conserve endangered and threatened species. It publishes the bimonthly magazine *National Wildlife*.

Natural Resources Defense Council (NRDC)
40 W. Twentieth St., New York, NY 10011
(212) 727-2700 • fax: (212) 727-1773
e-mail: nrdcinfo@nrdc.org
Web site: www.nrdc.org

The NRDC is a nonprofit organization with more than four hundred thousand members. It uses laws and science to protect the environment, including wildlife and wild places. NRDC publishes the quarterly magazine *OnEarth* (formerly *Amicus Journal*) and hundred of reports, including *Development and Dollars* and the annual report *Testing the Waters.*

Pew Center on Global Climate Change
2101 Wilson Blvd., Ste. 550, Arlington, VA 22201
(703) 516-4146 • fax: (703) 841-1422
Web site: www.pewclimate.org

The Pew Center is a nonpartisan organization dedicated to educating the public and policy makers about the causes and potential consequences of global climate change and informing them of ways to reduce the emissions of greenhouse gases. Its reports include *Designing a Climate-Friendly Energy Policy* and *The Science of Climate Change.*

Political Economy Research Center (PERC)
2048 Analysis Dr., Ste. A, Bozeman, MT 59718
(406) 587-9591
e-mail: perc@perc.org
Web site: www.perc.org

PERC is a nonprofit research and educational organization that seeks market-oriented solutions to environmental problems. The center holds a variety of conferences and provides educational material on environmental issues. It publishes the quarterly newsletter *PERC Reports*, commentaries, research studies, and policy papers, including "Economic Growth and the State of Humanity" and "The National Forests: For Whom and for What?"

Rainforest Action Network (RAN)
221 Pine St., Ste. 500, San Francisco, CA 94104
(415) 398-4404 • fax: (415) 398-2732
e-mail: rainforest@ran.org
Web site: www.ran.org

RAN works to preserve the world's rain forests through activism that addresses the logging and importation of tropical timber, cattle ranching in rain forests, and the rights of indigenous rain forest peoples. It also seeks to educate the public about the environmental effects of tropical hardwood logging. RAN's publications include the monthly *Action Report* and the semiannual *World Rainforest Report.*

Reason Foundation
3415 S. Sepulveda Blvd., Ste. 400, Los Angeles, CA 90034
(310) 391-2245 • fax: (310) 391-4395
Web site: www.reason.org

The Reason Foundation is a national research and educational organization that explores and promotes public policy based on rationality and freedom. The Reason Foundation's think tank—the Reason Public Policy Institute—promotes choice, competition, and a free-market economy as the foundation for human progress. The Reason Foundation publishes the monthly *Reason Magazine.*

Sierra Club
85 Second St., 2nd Fl., San Francisco, CA 94105-3441
(415) 977-5500 • fax: (415) 977-5799
e-mail: information@sierraclub.org
Web site: www.sierraclub.org

The Sierra Club is a grassroots organization with chapters in every state of the union. It promotes the protection and conservation of natural resources. The organization maintains separate committees on air quality, global environment, and solid waste, among other environmental concerns, to help achieve its goals. It publishes books, fact sheets, the bimonthly magazine *Sierra*, and the *Planet* newsletter, which appears several times a year.

Union of Concerned Scientists (UCS)
Two Brattle Sq., Cambridge, MA 02238
(617) 547-5552 • fax: (617) 864-9405

e-mail: ucs@ucsusa.org
Web site: www.ucsusa.org

UCS aims to advance responsible public policy in areas where science and technology play important roles. Its programs emphasize transportation reform, arms control, safe and renewable energy technologies, and sustainable agriculture. UCS publications include the twice-yearly magazine *Catalyst*, the quarterly newsletter *Earthwise*, and the reports "Greener SUVs" and "Greenhouse Crisis: The American Response".

Worldwatch Institute
1776 Massachusetts Ave. NW, Washington, DC 20036-1904
(202) 452-1999 • fax: (202) 296-7365
e-mail: worldwatch@worldwatch.org
Web site: www.worldwatch.org

Worldwatch Institute is a nonprofit public policy research organization dedicated to informing the public and policy makers about emerging global problems and trends and the complex links between the environment and the world economy. Its publications include *Vital Signs*, issued every year; the bimonthly magazine *World Watch*; the Environmental Alert series; and numerous policy papers, including "Unnatural Disasters" and "City Limits: Putting the Brakes on Sprawl."

Bibliography of Books

Kenny Ausubel	*Restoring the Earth: Visionary Solutions from the Bioneers.* Oakland, CA: H.J. Kramer, 1997.
Kenny Ausubel and J.P. Harpignies, eds.	*Ecological Medicine.* San Francisco: Sierra Club, 2004.
Kenny Ausubel and J.P. Harpignies, eds.	*Nature's Operating Instructions: The True Biotechnologies.* San Francisco: Sierra Club, 2004.
Ronald Bailey	*Liberation Biology: The Moral and Scientific Defense of the Biotech Revolution.* Amherst, NY: Prometheus, 2005.
Maude Barlow and Tony Clarke	*Blue Gold: The Fight to Stop the Corporate Theft of the World's Water.* New York: New Press, 2002.
Wilfred Beckerman	*A Poverty of Reason: Sustainable Development and Economic Growth.* Oakland, CA: Independent Institute, 2002.
Harvey Blatt	*America's Environmental Report Card.* Cambridge, MA: MIT Press, 2005.
Lester R. Brown	*Eco-Economy: Building an Economy for the Earth.* New York: Norton, 2003.
Lester R. Brown	*Plan B: Rescuing a Planet Under Stress and a Civilization in Trouble.* New York: Norton, 2003.

Lester R. Brown, Janet Larsen, and Bernie Fischlowitz-Roberts	*The Earth Policy Reader*. New York: Norton, 2002.
Helen Caldicott	*The New Nuclear Danger*. New York: New Press, 2004.
Fritjof Capra	*Hidden Connections: A Science for Sustainable Living*. New York: Anchor, 2004.
Rachel Carson	*Silent Spring*. 40th anniversary ed. Boston: Houghton Mifflin, 2002.
Christopher D. Cook	*Diet for a Dead Planet: How the Food Industry Is Killing Us*. New York: New Press, 2004.
Guy Dauncey and Patrick Mazza	*Stormy Weather: 101 Solutions to Global Climate Change*. Gabriola Island, BC: New Society, 2001.
Paul Driessen	*Eco-Imperialism: Green Power, Black Death*. Bellevue, WA: Merril, 2003.
Richard Ellis	*The Empty Ocean*. Washington, DC: Shearwater, 2003.
E Magazine	*Green Living: The* E Magazine *Handbook for Living Lightly on the Earth*. New York: Plume, 2005.
Christopher Essex and Ross McKittrick	*Taken by Storm: The Troubled Science, Policy and Politics of Global Warming*. Toronto: Key Porter, 2003.

Dave Foreman — *Rewilding North America*. Washington, DC: Island, 2004.

R. Allen Freeze — *The Environmental Pendulum: A Quest for the Truth About Toxic Chemicals, Human Health, and Environmental Protection*. Berkeley and Los Angeles: University of California Press, 2000.

Ross Gelbspan — *Boiling Point: How Politicians, Big Oil and Coal, Journalists and Activists are Fueling the Climate Crisis*. New York: Basic Books, 2004.

Elizabeth Grossman — *High Tech Trash: Digital Devices, Hidden Toxins, and Human Health*. Washington, DC: Island, 2006.

Stephen F. Hayward — *Index of Leading Environmental Indicators, 2005*. Sacramento, CA: Pacific Research Institute, 2005.

Peter Huber — *Hard Green: Saving the Environment from Environmentalists*. New York: Basic Books, 2000.

Peter Huber and Mark P. Mills — *The Bottomless Well: The Twilight of Fuel, the Virtue of Waste, and Why We Will Never Run Out of Energy*. New York: Basic Books, 2005.

Derrick Jensen and George Draffan — *Strangely Like War: The Global Assault on Forests*. White River, VT: Chelsea Green, 2003.

Bjørn Lomborg — *Global Crises, Global Solution*. Cambridge: Cambridge University Press, 2004.

Bjørn Lomborg	*The Skeptical Environmentalist: Measuring the Real State of the World.* Cambridge: Cambridge University Press, 2001.
William McDonough and Michael Braungart	*Cradle to Cradle: Remaking the Way We Make Things.* New York: North Point, 2002.
Ed McGaa	*Nature's Way: Native Wisdom for Living in Balance with the Earth.* San Francisco: HarperSanFrancisco, 2004.
Patrick J. Michaels	*Meltdown: The Predictable Distortion of Global Warming by Scientists, Politicians, and the Media.* Washington, DC: Cato Institute, 2004.
Henry I. Miller and Gregory Conko	*The Frankenfood Myth: How Protests and Politics Threaten the Biotech Revolution.* Westport, CT: Praeger, 2004.
Jim Motavalli	*Feeling the Heat: Dispatches from the Frontlines of Climate Change.* New York: Routledge, 2004.
Jim Motavalli	*Forward Drive: The Race to Build Clean Cars for the Future.* San Francisco: Sierra Club, 2001.
David Orr	*The Last Refuge: Patriotism, Politics, and the Environment in an Age of Terror.* Washington, DC: Island, 2004.
Dixie Lee Ray	*Environmental Overkill: Whatever Happened to Common Sense?* Washington, DC: Regnery Gateway, 1993.

Jeremy Rifkin	*The Hydrogen Economy*. New York: Putnam, 2002.
Joseph J. Romm	*The Hype About Hydrogen*. Washington, DC: Island, 2004.
S. Fred Singer	*Climate Policy*. Palo Alto, CA: Hoover Institution, 2000.
S. Fred Singer	*Hot Talk, Cold Science: Global Warming's Unfinished Debate*. Oakland, CA: Independent Institute, 1999.
Rory Spowers	*Rising Tides: A History of the Environmental Revolution and Visions for an Ecological Age*. Edinburgh, Scotland: Canongate, 2002.
Bruce Sterling	*Tomorrow Now: Envisioning the Next Fifty Years*. New York: Random House, 2003.
David Suzuki and Holly Dressel	*From Naked Ape to Superspecies: Humanity and the Global Ecocrisis*. Vancouver, BC: Greystone, 2005.
James Trefil	*Human Nature: A Blueprint for Managing the Earth—by People, for People*. New York: Owl, 2005.
Edward O. Wilson	*The Future of Life*. New York: Vintage, 2003.

Index